ONLY THOUGHTS

Philosophy of Everything

NECESSITY

SUJAL SAHU (S.S)

Chennai • Bangalore

CLEVER FOX PUBLISHING
Chennai, India

Published by CLEVER FOX PUBLISHING 2023
Copyright © Sujal Sahu 2023

All Rights Reserved.
ISBN: 978-93-56483-44-6

This book has been published with all reasonable efforts taken to make the material error-free after the consent of the author. No part of this book shall be used, reproduced in any manner whatsoever without written permission from the author, except in the case of brief quotations embodied in critical articles and reviews.

The Author of this book is solely responsible and liable for its content including but not limited to the views, representations, descriptions, statements, information, opinions and references ["Content"]. The Content of this book shall not constitute or be construed or deemed to reflect the opinion or expression of the Publisher or Editor. Neither the Publisher nor Editor endorse or approve the Content of this book or guarantee the reliability, accuracy or completeness of the Content published herein and do not make any representations or warranties of any kind, express or implied, including but not limited to the implied warranties of merchantability, fitness for a particular purpose. The Publisher and Editor shall not be liable whatsoever for any errors, omissions, whether such errors or omissions result from negligence, accident, or any other cause or claims for loss or damages of any kind, including without limitation, indirect or consequential loss or damage arising out of use, inability to use, or about the reliability, accuracy or sufficiency of the information contained in this book.

FOR

THE ABSOLUTE

Chapters

1. Motive of The Book — 1
   - Answer to all old question
   - Eliminating philosophy
   - Continuation through my books

2. What's Real and What Matters? — 3
   - What matter to whom
   - What is real
   - Concept of relative
   - Example of relative
   - The delusion of unreal
   - Nonsense - the bullshit, relative and relative bullshit

3. What Is a Thought? — 11
   - How would you define a thought?
   - Thought or thoughts?
   - What they depend on?
   - Circumstances and exploration

4. All Thoughts One and The Same — 15
   - Categories of thoughts?
   - Nonsense on the name of categories
   - Thoughts just as a necessity
   - No contradiction in reality
   - One of the biggest relative bullshits – good and bad

5. What Is Knowledge? — 21
   - Knowledge - an absolute thing

- Difference between knowledge and just information
- Defining 'terms'

6. Types of People on The Bases of Thoughts   25
    - Bases of categorization
    - Thinker
    - Normal
    - Default
    - Retard
    - Renovated retard

7. Necessities of Every Brain   53
    - Symmetry
    - New
    - Space
    - Smooth and shinny
    - Food and sex
    - Partial dependency
    - Biases which can't be Broken

8. Science Gets Retarded Because of
   Continuation of Different Fields of Philosophy   77
    - Philosophy – only thoughts
    - Science – only progressive
    - Nonsense on the name of different field of philosophy
    - Nonsense on science through philosophy
    - An example of relative bullshit philosophy
    - Progress is just done by science and its people

9. Justice Is Relative Bullshit   83
    - What is the biggest crime?

- What are the bases of difference
- Nothing is more or less than progress and retardness
- Necessity can be both progressive and retarding
- Survival of retards on the name of justice
- Example of relative bullshit laws
- How all of it going to end
- Someone should not be retarded because of laws if overall progressive

10. Equality Is Nonsense   95
    - Only retard talk about equality
    - We are not equal
    - Retard's delusion of overall progress
    - Slavery – it's lies and nonsense
    - Socialism is retardness
    - Male and female are not equal
    - Most of the population is miserable and going to die miserably anyway
    - Examples of prevailing retardness on the name of equality

11. Democracy – Rule of Renovated Retards   111
    - Majority retard the progress through democracy
    - Something to reduce the retardness of democracy
    - Democracy is not a progressive system
    - No difference between democracy and monarch system

12. What Now?   119
    - Final talks
    - The chart of necessities
    - The delusion of survival without benefits of the progress

Chapter 1

Motive of The Book

This book is written so that people can understand what is something to think on and what is something which is so worthless that even thinking on that and them calling them worthless is also waste of time. As per today's world this book is very important because this century will lead to the biggest transformation in the history of the whole world, though every century has something special (from last few centuries) but this time is best period for progress in the sense of achieving ultimate progress and for the people who lead progress and also for some people who are in the ways of progress. This book will tell you what exactly is real, knowledge and absolute which lead to progress and this book in not fairy-tale (nonsense) which most of the people in the world is use to, this is not for at least 85% of the population. This book will help you to understand your own thoughts, other people thoughts, what exactly thoughts are and how they work. Through this book you will understand not only how to create knowledge and how to apply it but also what knowledge govern all other kind of knowledge. The most important motive is that to identify the people and other things which are in way of progress and thinking which is in the way of progress.

From so many years people are just dragging the old philosophy for no reason other then for nonsense. Let me tell you all the useful things from useful philosophy have been changed into science. But still many people believe that there are many philosophies like Axiology, Metaphysics, Logic, Aesthetics, Epistemology, Ethics and Political philosophy etc. make sense and can be used, as you may know all of the branches of philosophy have contradictory thing which obviously shows they are not useful at all at the first place. To clear every thing once and for all and to make sure that you can all understand on your own what is progressive I will explain every single aspect from which philosophy originated whiling using science which has no contradictions starting with this book to bust all bullshit base and explaining basic necessities then explaining theory of every thing (connectivity) in the second book which is an continuation of this book in aesthetics but it has the theory of every thing which is an physics theory to explain everything and then in end solving all the prior unsolved paradoxes in the third book. So, you never ever have to read philosophy because it is nothing more than nonsense when useful things have been already taken out of it and there is no need of continuation of different field of philosophy.

The only reason I have written this book because there is no book which clear things what I am going to explain and that basic knowledge is necessary for reading 'Connectivity' and 'Solution of all unsolved paradoxes. These books are written in 2018 to 2022 and published simultaneously for progress and the absolute.

Chapter 2

What's Real and What Matters?

If you are familiar with philosophy than you may have read about different criteria to identify what's real and what matters but then you must have realize till now that what most of the philosopher talk about is not at all easy to apply nor seem like it is really applicable always and very few philosopher really talk or talked about something which lead to progress, though they are the only philosopher who are important as they create or created knowledge but then there are many people who consider them self as philosopher but talk nonsense while retarding the progress, off curse most of the people are retard too so they just can't differentiate and this book is not for those people who simply a lost call (which is majority). Now I want you to understand overall real thing's matter but nonsense in particular (reference system which can't be explained or understood) matter too, the only difference is group of people, real things matters for the progress to the people who lead to progress or cope up with it and only nonsense in particular matter a lot to the people who retard the progress and that type of people always have been more in number throughout the history and still they are more in number but the best part is this is last century for them.

But then what is real which matters and lead to progress and how to identify? Identifying reality is very easy if something is real it will not be about nonsense (mostly a language system or any action which doesn't refer to anything, we will define the three ways to achieve nonsense afterwards) nor it has anything to do with it, if something is nonsensical it will be nonsense and there is no other thing then reality, but then what is nonsense? It's very easy to know what is nonsense as it is nothing more than about delusion (thinking to be able to think even though not able to thinking about something or on something, mostly a language system) which always have seemingly (or allegedly) opposite - delusion (if relative or relative bullshit) which reveals it's self-contradictory nature and shows how opposite contradict each other and off course reality can't be self-contradictory and real (absolute) thing doesn't have any opposite thing which can contradict them so whatsoever opposite word you know you must understand either one of them is for real or not even one of them is for real, for example small and big look these both words are nonsense as they are not absolute. if I say think small? What do you think is small or big or anything at all? Of course, not as they are not for real, even though you think you can come up with a range (open or closed) or limit (lower or above) for example in male height above 5ft8inch every male is big and below that is small then also when I ask you to think of a small male, can you think of all height measurement at the same time? Of course not even when you think or see a particular height let say 5ft10inch then also you are not thinking nonsense (relative) for real it is absolute and again you can't think nonsense to be for real, you would have thought of this even when I would have said think or see a 5ft10inch man, so I want you to understand only absolute thing can be formed and can be result of two or more different things and there is no way you can think nonsense for real (relative) but off course you can be in a delusion that you can think nonsense for real but indeed the only reality is you can't.

Nonsense which is supposedly is for things varies from person to person, if every person claims to defines something in just his or her way that simply means it nonsense (mostly relative or relative bullshit) but then how and what exactly make's nonsense self-contradictory? Reality is absolute it doesn't changes (other than your own thinking) from what's you think and what you believe and doesn't depend upon just your observation because just person's observation is not something to rely on because a person can be biased while making observation or can neglect something while making observation or may not have proper tools to observe, but nonsense thing through observation of things, through definition and as per people opinion show there self contradictory nature unlike real observation and explanation of real things which remains absolute and most importantly they show how insignificant nonsense thing are whether a person consider any part of any nonsense in any way or doesn't consider it at all it just doesn't make any different in progress but instead of that consideration of it lead to an loop of retardness (other nonsense) and becomes obstacle in the path of progress for example whether you have read philosophy (excluding which has become science) or not before, it still has nothing to do with progress and there will be no product which you can't create or no function which you can't carry on if you haven't read philosophy. Nonsense thing are not for absolute which is obvious but because of which they doesn't have any real definition too (to refer to something) and top of all one must remember person can only think he or she can understand nonsense but nobody can understand nonsense for real and they are not unreal thinking for real (they are just terminologies or definitions in language system mostly) nor anybody can think of nonsense in absolute sense to make 'unreal' real, nobody can think unreal as there is no such thing like that (and unreal is nonsense), a person can just think that he/she know nonsense but can't think of any nonsense in particular in itself.

For a person who really want progress should not even try to look at nonsense even for anybody personally because knowing a nonsense can cause delusion which in particular can be problematic because the people who are very deep in this delusion can't happy nor can be progressive as they always suffer from the thinking that they lack something this happens because a person only lack those things which is in his/her brain (whether in term of absolute or something which they think they can think of but they can't think of that indeed for real which means nonsense) but not in there reach and as I just told you what nonsense are. Hence, the more a person try to solve and try to differentiate (to find more of it) or try to think on nonsense then that person suffer more from the felling of lacking and more the person detach himself/herself from progress after all how you can have something or understand or explain something which is not for real at the first place. To be clear about one thing nonsense is synonym to unreal (and you can say visa versa) and thus both meaning is exactly the same if a person tells you otherwise then that person is just creating nonsense (mostly relative or relative bullshit).

One of thing which retard people think they understand is nonsense examples (mostly of relative and sometimes of relative bullshit) which now a days known as metaphor, references, analogy etc. which means they think two different scenarios has somehow become nonsenses (have something to do with each other, what? I don't know nor does they) to each other and to create a nonsense. First this is impossible as one can understand retards are just in delusion of thinking that they can think even when they can't (obviously can't comprehend himself/herself while believing they can i.e., nonsense for real), which is just retard thinking and saying that they can relate something with something, but reality is we can't as we can just have two different thing/circumstances together in our brain which is not nonsense (relative) so that they can't interchange there position/quality/property or something else with each other and simantaneouly become both of the thing at same time while still maintaining separate identity (which is being relative while being not which is an contradiction to the term relative which shows indeed there is no such thing as relative) and even if people try to make something nonsense (relative) or a term (bullshit) which I exactly can't think off nor you can, then of course that will contradictory always to it self at the first place even before you show contradiction to any thing which is real and we know reality is not contradictory (contradiction is just to show that an given term is meaningless or you can say to show it is relative or relative bullshit or nonsense) and nor we can think contradictory as all of us know we can't focus/think of two different things in the way I mentioned above and nor any two different scenarios while considering them can be interchangeable but yet maintains same identity. If that would happen than also things have to be nonsense (relative at least) first, so to have nonsense (relative) you need nonsense (relative) first to have a nonsense for real to make sense like that (relativity) which is in self is nonsense (relative and also relative to other relative so overall just nonsense).

So reality is absolute not nonsense nor is for nonsense, just to give more example, a retard can given an example like this book is hard like an iron or this book is hard like an diamond or this book shine like an diamond, now in these nonsense (relative) example most probably an retard would like the relative of this book shine like an diamond (and even would think this book is better without thing why other than just some relative bullshit) even though it doesn't mean more than nonsense and you can only think of either diamond or book but retards will chose that most probably because he/she is thinking about diamond and it's TIR and retard's always give example like these as they doesn't mean anything and they doesn't understand anything nor they want too, but they may want to have little bit stimulation or pseudo experience (mostly words are the only considerable money for retards). That's why so many retard people talk so much of nonsense even which can have opposite and contradictory for the same nonsense (relative or relative bullshit) and some people go with some so-called point of view and some with other, this happens as these retards who just have nothing more than nodding heads doesn't understand that at the first place nor the person who claim to explain nonsense for real understand that himself/herself nor they them self, after all that's why retards are mostly very idiotic who retard progress very significantly. So, we doesn't need a base nor we can have a base to point out nonsense for real (relative or relative bullshit, specially hollow term or sentence) as we can't think nonsense for real hence we can't address nonsense (unreal) to make sense therefore we can't oppose it or support it with real (and that's why retards does think they can and want too oppose or support that), we can just point out any nonsense in the sense what I talked earlier so that to prove that the bases of it is basically baseless which means we just point out what retards consider as an base of something or nonsense as something basically they not really considering anything they are just fooling around.

Now let's define the three different types or different way of creating nonsense- relative, relative bullshit, bullshit. First, in this book if you see anywhere bullshit it just does not mean unreal thing, as unreal thing doesn't exist nor anybody can think unreal for thing (I am not all bothered to create a new term for that) but it is synonym to that (not in the sense like people try to define or identify unreal for real to make sense), it just means (mostly) an 'hollow' terminology (its a term which quiet famous and many times before have been used as synonym to my term bullshit, though its origin is nonsense of representation) which is hollow from inside (doesn't refer to anything real), though term bullshit (or hollow) can also be used for overall sentence to refer to that it is nonsense which can be relative and relative bullshit also. Overall bullshit (or any nonsense) people think they can think about a term or action (in the sense that it represent or refer something) but they can't think about it in reality but remain in delusion that means something (which they doesn't know what) so they remain in confusion always and that word or idea always make confusion and can be used for opposed and support of any thing as that thing doesn't mean anything anyway (though that's the case for any nonsense) hence really can't be opposed or supported in reality hence that term in self is great thing for retards to oppose and support (in the sense, used for being in delusion and creating delusion in retards - that they can think of that even though they can't about that). And all of this means retardness and ignorance which of course originates from by idiots.

Another term which I will use overall is relative bullshit (here bullshit is to refer to part or a term of the statement not the whole statement) in which I think I am clear about both of them separately, but I still want to clear about relative which is basically something (language is mostly the way) which in itself as whole doesn't refer to anything i.e. overall bullshit (statement) but doesn't have the individual component as bullshit, example we took before most of them were relative bullshit or just relative, if something is just relative but very less relative or bit relative (or at least not 100% relative) i.e. it is itself is managed to refer to a relation or correlation which in itself is not absolute than it can lead to progress but bullshit or relative bullshit can't ever. All relative terms or definition overall are hollow (bullshit) in the sense of being relative (i.e., contradictory overall for reference as they don't really refer to anything but people can make allegation) but not all hollow term or sentence are relative but of course if person try to explained unexplainable (in language or otherwise) obviously they will just make it relative bullshit. Relative bullshit is simply the combination of both relative and bullshit as components but overall, it also doesn't refer to anything, hence it is also overall bullshit. So overall creation of nonsense causes delusion.

Note – Delusion simply means one think he/she can think about a term or something about something or just as overall thing but indeed he/she is really not thinking of that in reference or any way but is just thinking that he/she can think even though he/she can't. Delusion can't mean more or less than that.

Just clear everything up I will give example of all nonsense which will be about famous nonsense, which are as follows-

1. Relative- A simple statement like 'lines on your palm changes according to your action' is relative. In this every component indeed refer to things like hand (obviously if you got hand), lines at palm, action also refer to things but most important problem with that is action is not defined absolutely for the whole statement as any thing is an action and many thing can be considered as your action, for example if you kick a ball then that can cause so many changes and changes after changes will occur so even if that doesn't hit something directly still it can be considered your action (hence action for sure is relative and its relation for the sentence is relative) and hence overall statement like that become nonsense (bullshit). One reason why people can consider the statement bit relative rather than 100% is because your action i.e., folding of your palm skin while you do something and your skin type or condition is also can be considered as your action but obviously even if they are able to make relation or correctional still it is not absolute, but most importantly sentence was not made that way hence sentence is 100% relative, though you can't think nonsense (unreal) for real or to make sense, so you may on your own can make an absolute relation while trying to thinking indeed or may be not because you want to be delusion and then you show retardness (and then live and die miserably) .

2. Relative bullshit – A simple statement for this would be "this line at lower center of your hand is the representation of your life time and it is governed by whoochawho -a god". In this statement the direct bullshit is the representation of line as any way to something or as something as no way anything can represent something but even if the sentence would be like line refer to life time, then also it is bullshit as life time is direct bullshit in itself but people may try to make

statement in which can consider a liner thing for accountability and try to use it for account life in any way which in itself would be relative bullshit and only best thing possible is bit significantly relative for a graph for life expectancy projection while considering overall well being as it's too much of accountability to consider all parameters even if you know what progression formula you should use (which is absolute). Another direct bullshit here is whoochawho which I called god, in this whoochawho in itself doesn't refer to anything but even if I say it is god still is not refer to anything directly because the most famous definition of it is something which people pray to and who people believe created the universe, so just because you used something than it doesn't mean it is referring to something though while using that term people are most likely to create relative bullshit at the first place but important thing from that to understand is if a term which refer to something indeed then also that can be directly used as bullshit like the term 'created' if person has no knowledge and information about that.

One thing to be very clear about i.e., if a person tries to create relative of relative bullshit, then it will be relative bullshit only (though for sure that will give more scope of creating nonsense). And relative of relative is relative until and unless taken as claim of being something in particular. Something which is relative can be given a name (to say it's a thing or something) and then used directly in any scenario which will be relative bullshit.

3. Direct bullshit – A very simple example of this will be '5 is a lucky number'. Yes indeed 5 can refer to something and that what's makes an number meaningful but that doesn't mean saying just a number is not bullshit and overall bullshit as lucky doesn't refer to anything, quiet frankly lucky is one of mostly rare term which is direct bullshit though people can use it is with relative bullshit like good or bad to act like it is not direct bullshit which overall would be relative bullshit but ironically it is one of term which idiots are not bothered to make relative bullshit to retards to be more delusional as this is one of the oldest term. But from above examples you can understand many times even worst idiots don't use direct bullshit and it is the least used nonsense and even idiot or retard can figure what is direct bullshit many times.

Note – Something which is not nonsense indeed can be nonsense for a particular person because they person doesn't understand that something from reference or that thing in itself and then most probably claim to understand that after some nonsense or by making nonsenses. For example, a person A can refer to my books in a conversation with person B, but B claim to understand what I have written (irrespective of he/she has read my books or not) even though when that person B don't understand anything and just talk nonsense on the name of my books.

At last I would like to say there is no such thing like logic other than something which is not nonsense as obviously you can say logic is sensible then any thing which is sensible which is basically anything in itself or any system which refer to anything is logic but obviously nonsense are there to not to make sense for anything or to anything.

Chapter 3

What Is a Thought?

Ask yourself how would you define a thought? Would you define something like a thought is something which is result of thinking or while we use any of our senses, we have thought about something particular or thought is nothing more than an impulse in a brain or thought is something which can't be defined. Let me tell you one thing in whatsoever way you will define thought it will be useless because there is nothing like thought, there is no particular thing exist which we can define just as a term thought, so why did I ask you this question? Answer is that I want you to understand - thought don't exist just as term but it exist as a category (every category is a term but visa versa is not possible) which I like to call thoughts as they are not same in terms of how much they are in quantity, quality or configuration (as of a just term) but yet one category with doesn't break, but then you may say why I use plural not singular verb? Answer is very simple I don't want to be bound to have a single particular unit (especially in term of configuration) to be same to define the category for example if I show you an image of ocean and image of pound you will say its water but water is a not an particular category which has a particular unit defined at the smallest particular level i.e. H^2O is ice (solid state of water) also but with different configuration in between, so basically I don't want to have problem of configuration changing my category or creating sub category and I don't want any sub category to make my category which can change the whole category or can make it contradictory in the sense even when an sub category is not present the category is still same, so at end I would say thoughts exist always until and unless you are alive as brain impulse but I can't be sure to say that for thought even when I define it as a category. This way I can always remind you of exact meaning and how terms can be made contradiction free.

What are thoughts and what they depend on? To explain that I want you to understand thoughts are nothing more than motion of stuff so there is flow of thoughts which can't be broken in something to create just something particular which you would able to call thought. And to understand what that flow depends on; you must understand accountability of motion of something just depend upon three things
1. what it is in itself?
2. Where it is going?
3. What are the things which makes its circumstances?

For example flow of water in a river can't be broken down is something particular like H2O to call water and it's flow and we dissolve that problem overall by having an breaking limit by using the word thoughts, so category like that can be only be divided till the thing which we have is something which will be (always) a same category but yet can be different in quantity, quality or configuration and just like flow of water in a river depend upon where that river is, what direction it is going and what is the structure/content of river is, same way your thoughts depend on three thing
1. Your circumstances (considering whole scenario which you are part of).
2. What are you thinking about (What you explore – only for living being).
3. What is your brain structure is like.

Those are the three things which decide in which way a person will behave because a person behaviour is nothing more than results of thoughts. But than you may ask what is the difference between exploring something and something to be your circumstance. To understand the difference, one must self-evaluate oneself that circumstances are general but what a person chose to explore is not at all general, one can only chose what to explore from his/her circumstances only. If you wonder what does exploring particular thing means? Then answer is very simple when you ignore all other thing from your circumstances except one and react or process that stimuli (showing more creativity), that is exploring (ignoring simply means not reacting or processing a stimulus further more than just what it is as reception, you can ignore something only if it's in your circumstance). An example of ignoring is listening to a foreign language, you do listen what somebody is saying but you don't understand that and hence easier it become to ignore that sound and you more easily forget what was the sound like, the same thing you do for the language you understand while you are thinking on something as you can't stop your receptors from working. So, an ignorant know what he/she is indeed ignoring, of course not exactly as they ignore it just at the moment so they don't explore that thing further than just as a reception (which we can call superficial).

But from this one may think a person who is rich for sure will have better circumstances than a poor person so the probability of poor person to explore something great become very less, if you think in that way let me tell the answer is no, it seem like people's circumstances vary a lot for learning knowledge but that's not the reality because for something to be called a part of person circumstance it is not necessary to that person that he/she can access (if not owning) that thing through all senses, using of one sense is more than enough to make some thing part of your circumstances, though most of people may think without able to access something properly or accessing something with only one sense how come a person can explore that thing if you think like that then, first- you forgot we are talking knowledge (specially learning basic science with minimal this is definitely the most easiest thing), second- you may have forget once this planet have nothing rather than rocks and water and some other species, what you have today, all the thing which surround you, around you for progress is man made only and they made all these thing out of this planet only, third – When you get an idea about what other necessities are and that there can be something particular for use in something particular it become lot more easier to create similar thing without exploring the prior (particular) things properly. So, if one really what to create something better than something or want to copy something, too much information not at all need it depend on the person whether person really want to create something which led to progress and fulfil the purpose. And remember there is nothing which a person can't understand correctly by himself/herself if he/she don't

1. assume
2. ignore
3. act like biased
4. use experience (i.e., to create some relative or relative bullshit).

It's very important to understand experience has nothing to do with person will be able to create something new or not directly because experience is based on the reality of past or someone else reality it always going to differ from reality of present, your reality, and from the other stuff which is not at all included as part of new creation and I already told you thing are not relative or relative bullshit and if you just use something (as it is) which exist before hand then you didn't created anything new and again nonsense doesn't create new. The people who are highly experienced and think it will help them in any way other then knowing what they know beforehand (also in knowing whether they are retard or not) or in knowing that something particular can be connect to other stuff (or knowledge) to create new, then they does suffer from delusion, than for sure they have a delusion of thinking they know something more than others in terms of creating something new which will never help them instead of that because of that they will just delay creation of anything new even they have created something new beforehand and feeling of being highly experienced will stop them to create something new again because they become highly biased about pre existing things at particular state. And it is obvious if your thinking off or doing something absolute you can't relate it with another thing so basically when you think of using of or use experience to claim something new is created because there was something other then that things which you have created was there before hand than you just think unreal or you would try to make things relative which indeed you can't to make sense, you can just think you can but indeed you can't in reality.

There is no doubt in that the people who make something new or came up with new thoughts which are helpful in progress or lead to progress or people who just cope up with progress rise from anywhere. Now for sure you must not be thinking there is an huge difference in peoples circumstances for knowledge but then you may think what drive us to chose particular thing? Though I will talk about that in the whole book later then also most important is brain structure now when I say brain structure don't think some people have very great brain structure and some just don't, you are not born at particular brain structure which makes you a genius or is rigid, it changes with what you explore more often, you may say that is what we started with but that's what the reality is because in our childhood we try to explored everything but then we start focusing more on some particular things, so answer for that is - that depended on which type of person you are (or which type you are becoming more and more while you explore something or want to explore something or nonsense) and that's what the next thing we are going to talk about but before that, can we categorize thoughts? Answer is no.

Chapter 4

All Thoughts One and The Same

Most of people think thoughts have categories like good, bad, right, wrong, positive, negative etc. But let me tell you one simple thing these categories just don't exist. First- because they are relative bullshit, second- there is no origin which lead to these categories, I mean who told you that on what basis one particular kind of thoughts should fall on this or that category (considering thoughts have sub category by witch magic and obviously thoughts can't be sub category), there is no bases on which you can categorise thoughts, if you think you can categorise thoughts on bases of shitty mythology then let me tell you all the mythologies are baseless and worthless hence lead to no progress and only talk about nonsense, but for sure it's impossible to lead to any conclusion through which we can define thoughts through which we can put some thoughts in one category. The most important thing one must remember if a category doesn't mean anything before hand then it can't mean any thing after hand for example if I say that I have good, right, ethical, moral product can you tell me what product that is, do you have slight bit of an idea what it is? Definitely you don't know. One may say you really give me a product I will tell you which category it falls in but if you can't tell anything before then how you can tell anything after, which simply mean it is a relative bullshit (same is the case for any thoughts to be called any thing). Obviously a example of use of categories would be saying I got an product which has glass which converges light rays, so it can be spectacle which can be useful for person with myopia but even if that's not the case still it is not in any way contradictory to use of categories (considering that's a real category not nonsense).

Look meaningful category is not made by simply putting things together and giving a name, calling it category. Category are made when somethings have something common or same in between different configurations or things which is absolute not relative and obviously not direct bullshit. One example of famous relative bullshit is 'weird', sometimes people act like it is just a term, sometimes people act like it is a category, obviously it is not a term as it doesn't mean anything (refer to nothing real) and obviously it is not a category because it doesn't mean anything in any sense to define an absolute property to be same or in common in between different real things and because it is purely a relative bullshit, it is quiet famous today (nothing to wonder about that). One must understand retards try to say something is a category rather than just term because it increases the scope of relative or relative bullshit or adding direct bullshit (like saying something is a sub category of a category even though it doesn't full fill the main category definition), another thing which retards do is saying this category (even if it is not nonsense) is limited by some short nonsenses (or the thing which fall in that category) or no overlapping of categories because of something which would be nonsense. One more thing which people must understand is most of terms you know and think are just terms are most probably categories.

But then what to say about thoughts? Look as I earlier defined thoughts, you must have understood that to really define thinking we have to define thoughts not thought which is an category in itself without sub category which doesn't have any contradiction and even if a person say it can have sub categories still sub category doesn't changes category in itself so thoughts is an category so all thoughts (constitutes of the category thoughts) are same but not equal hence can very at quantity and quality or configuration in between but that doesn't changes the category (remember only all real sub categories together can make a category) and even if person try to have sub category of thoughts still sub category are based on category and category of thoughts have nothing which can be sub divided and specially meaningless sub categories can't make a meaningful category and can't be derived from meaningful category so in every sense good, bad, right, wrong, positive, negative have nothing to do with thoughts.

Overall thoughts can be defined as just necessities nothing more than that as necessities is an category which can take all category inside it or can have synonym as highest category as necessity is simply defined as definition of scenario (basically directly about interactions) which is generally lead to something particular and is an result of something particular which means in other words you can define every thoughts flow as an result of necessity and necessity in itself and I already told you they depend on only three thing what your circumstances are, what you explore, and what's your brain structure is like, so whenever I talk about necessities in this whole book I am talking about people necessities.

All the thoughts are same as a category, if they are thoughts. What I mean is that, at starting I told you the category of thoughts are unreal things which lead to no progress but then if that things are not thoughts, you must be thinking if something is not thoughts how come a person can think related to that thing or term? Again, answer is nobody in reality think of nonsense in the sense of reference, they just think they can think but they can't and overall, you can put real things in relative bullshit or relative or bullshit category which obviously not what a (real) category is (which refer to absolute things in between same or common). For example, if I say think good, can you think good? If you say yes, than let me tell you are not thinking good you are thinking of an circumstance which you are categorising as good without any absolute reason to call it good and you are doing that to create an category of good (relative bullshit), in the same way if I say think bad, positive, negative etc. you will think of an circumstance which you think fall in this or that so-called different categories of thought but in reality you can't think good, bad, right, wrong etc. and that not the only thing as I told you unreal thing are relative so the moment I say to think good, different people will imagine different circumstance which has nothing same or common, and even what is good for one-other can think it as bad and how come reality can self-contradictory and relative. That simply proves they are not real (so basically it is nonsense).

Though it's obvious you can't think of nonsense as for things because I just told you thoughts are based only on three thing which are the only real things and no nonsense can come in between as if everything is real than from where the nonsense (or unreal as people can say) can in or comes in between (considering people's claim that there can be unreal). For example, right now you are reading this, this is you circumstance and what you explore is this page now if I ask different people who have read this page or reading currently to image this book and this page all of the people will imagine same only (if can remember the whole or things which would same or common in between) after all this page is copy of something real and is real in itself. But let's take some examples to prove the contradictory nature of relative things first let's talk about good and bad, so let's consider pain, what you think pain is? If you think pain is bad or good then let me tell pain is nor good nor bad (just to say it's all are relative bullshit) there many different type of pain different people like without exception, no one in the world is there who don't like a particular kind of pain, if you work out you like pain while doing the work out, if you like spices you like the pain which spices gives as it is not taste but overall an pain connected experience, if you are thinker you like the pain of thinking again and again to fetch the result so you can create what nobody has ever created, if you like to be disciplined in particular way you may like particular pain in which you wanted to be disciplined, if you like the stimulation created by pain which excite you still it is pain only, if you got pain and somebody take care of you even though that person is the only one who gave you pain - you like that pain with combination of other stimulation, if you get pain because of inconvenience at something and it makes you desperate to take that thing and you got it - you like pain, if you got different kind of pain beforehand now which have increase your pain tolerance which helped you in particular situation and you know that then you like pain, after all pain is not just an experience through nothing more than a receptors nor just not an stimulation of one particular receptor and pain is an complex felling not just an bit of receptor stimulation otherwise very menial animal feel pain too which is definitely not the case, there is no doubt there are different receptor but there is no doubt they are just morphologically different but not in terms of creating impulse as all impulse are same of course some can be more intense than other but there is nothing from which we can differentiate any kind of different thought or action (which obviously need thinking) so that we can create relative bullshit category like good, bad, right, wrong, positive, negative etc., of course different in any thoughts means different form of impulse together by which I mean different configuration of neurons, ganglion cells and different configuration of impulse which are formed in them simantaneouly but they not changing in itself to be differentiated to create some opposite things nor opposite things exist, different types doesn't create anything which can be called opposite and definition of opposite is not absolute either, it is an relative bullshit or relative.

We just like stimulation of any particular receptor and overall, just particular thoughts to fulfil our necessities just like any other necessity fulfilling scenario. One must remember a person feel happy or sad when he/she think it is necessary to feel so according to fulfilment of necessities and person feels unhappy only if necessities are not fulfilled which result in different necessities which causes misery, if what happen to the person matches his/her necessities then it make person happy, though we are going to talk about common necessity of every brain without exception afterwards but the most important thing is a person feel sad at less stimulation but can't feel sad when having more stimulation which mean stimulation of different senses together and in terms of thoughts which we will talk about this later too (limits implied). Necessities are slowly shaped by the three factor which we talked about earlier, no sudden change in necessity can cause a permanent long-term change in overall necessity. At least something to change necessity overall need a month (or significant effect) in the sense of no direct induction of anything then at the best 3 months, why so? As it depended on memory a lot so something can really change thinking (especially by having more certain thoughts) by changing brain structure and something to be best in memory it should be remembered by you at following time 137131 from days to month to year, take them as necessary check point. After a year of checking, you remember it at above following time then for sure that thing have potentially changes your necessities but age matters in all this - obviously prior necessities.

Just like there is nothing like good and bad there is no such thing like some creative thought as every real thoughts are creative only (though some retard people have some relative bullshit definition of creativity or creative and obviously the mostly the important thing is more or less creative which obviously correlate to more or less thoughts), but most of the people just have thoughts that they have thoughts but in reality they don't have about real things which basically means retard people think they can think unreal (as they say) but reality (the only possible case) is they just can have thoughts that they can think unreal but indeed they doesn't think unreal (nonsense in the sense some thing or relation) so that's why they are not more creative or creative to solve emerging problem and many surveys says creative people know they are creative before hand for quiet a while that simply only means they are used to have thoughts and know they have thoughts about real thing to cope up with progress but the most people don't have thoughts about real things they just have thoughts of having thoughts of unreal thing which is mostly an hollow term, they never believe they are creative that obvious too as they never have a thoughts about real things properly so they can't create something new on there own at the first place or to cope up with progress.

Again, there is no such thing like good and bad then how come positive and negative, right and wrong can exist, specially if good and bad doesn't exist at the first place (as allegedly they have something to do with each other), there is only real thing exist and there is no categorization like that about thoughts or anything which is not nonsense. Basically, what people want to oppose or support they give it a term and then they say it should or should not happen or happen (or be done) because this is this (nonsense) which off course other retards can take as reasoning but that is nothing more that nonsense (mostly its relative or relative bullshit). Let's take an example let say a retard say you shouldn't do that 'x' thing because it is bad, then you may ask why it should not be done (to understand)? Then retards would answer you because it bad that's why it should not be done or will tell you so and so relative reason (which basically make no sense) and I already told you there is no relative example or reasoning exist so nothing can't be relative to word bad (to make sense) which in itself is a relative bullshit. If you will ask retard again what is bad and so what? Then retard will tell you it is bad so it should not be done but then why it is bad? Only because it should be done? But if that the case reasoning (which is relative bullshit) then for sure it doesn't make sense because if something shouldn't be done before hand then why to have other reasoning (relative) for it and how come there can be reasoning (relative) for it at the first place and why not anything about bad is absolute? The answer is because concept of bad is relative bullshit. From this you can understand all thoughts are one and same but there is no doubt that some thoughts are combination of many things which led to more progress and some thoughts can be better in term of how they led to progress and then there are retards who mostly just have thoughts that they have thoughts (they think they can think even when they can't) and obviously retards want to think they are progressive on the basis of some nonsense which of course retard the progress.

Chapter 5

What Is knowledge?

So, what is knowledge? It is very easy to answer, knowledge can't be nonsense so what is real must have governing knowledge behind it (and would be a knowledge in itself, if applicable) and as I told you earlier that all real thing is absolute so knowledge can't have exceptions or in other words knowledge can't be nonsense or in other word it should be real in itself not relative or relative bullshit or bullshit. The differentiation you must learn is every information (real thing, no relative bullshit or relative or bullshit is a reference to any information and they are only information In the sense of what system it is like a language system) is not always the governing knowledge which we will call just information but some information are absolute which are governing thing behind more than one thing and part of more than one thing which we will simply call knowledge- which is generally have been norm too, knowledge can be further be differentiated into sub knowledge and knowledge in which sub knowledge is knowledge only but for more particular scenarios (as per the definition of sub categories). So, one must remember after the application of knowledge the fetch result is not be knowledge it is information and from information one can only fetch information. Thus, every knowledge can fetch information but information can't fetch knowledge (Though can be knowledge in them self).

One thing I do want to be very clear about i.e. what to call as main knowledge and sub knowledge can depend on the person which no way hinder the progress (as it is just about the categorization conditions, though the top most category for any scenarios should be called knowledge) but it doesn't depend on the person what knowledge is, hence knowledge is not an relative bullshit or relative or bullshit, though this is also true for any information but obviously people can make them relative bullshit or relative or bullshit in sense of retardness like delusions etc. It is quiet obvious every knowledge can be defined as necessity as it is always be defined as nothing more than something has to do something with something or interaction or something (reality), hence necessities are synonym to information (which can be knowledge). Many times, people create relative bullshit out of information or necessities which is obviously not knowledge but many people present any such things like knowledge or just any information and start teaching that which is obviously not progressive.

For example, a person has done so and so (obviously referring to something), this is an information but not knowledge but if we say that person necessity because of the necessity of scenario is govern by so and so this make person do so and so it is the not knowledge still but this can be sub knowledge not the full knowledge because full knowledge will the three thing which govern every single human necessity. So, one must first seek for knowledge not for sub knowledge and at no condition for just information (which are not confined by knowledge) which doesn't lead to any progress. Lets take an another example counting is knowledge and let say there is 100 people in a particular area this is just information but if we say there only 100 because of so and so reason and if same condition will be there then same number of people will be there is a sub knowledge, so basically if we say these are the condition on which people living in area depend is sub knowledge and again every sub knowledge is necessity only not more than that but necessity of particular scenario because every thing depend on that sub knowledge of that scenario, so necessity in general can be defined as only information which is knowledge (which still is absolute but we don't subscribe to that) and all other are sub knowledge or just information.

One must ask himself/herself constantly what I am trying to learn is a knowledge, sub knowledge or just information (which lead to progress or not) and one must understand that knowledge is always very little and very small which is basically necessities only but can be defined in different scenario and to confine different information but meaning never changes, sub knowledge are lengthy and deep, particular on the topic whereas just information is mostly nothing more than big pile of stuff which doesn't lead to progress mostly for example terminologies (in term of writing, speaking and reading), terminologies can mostly be worthless anybody can give any term to anything thing or produce any hollow term which are obviously easy to remember because they are just very few configuration of very few alphabet (or something else) and similarly any information just about anything. Important thing is one understand something or not properly instead of just knowing the terminology and top of that what that person creates, modify and give or add value to. Most importantly to retarding people terminologies seem a great important deal.

I want to be clear about one thing i.e., terms or word as many renovated retards makes relative or relative bullshit out of it. First - terms are to refer to things not to represent them, so it is very important to understand any particular thing can only be represent by itself only to be really be represented, for example I only can represented by myself, second - something same or in common doesn't makes things equal, third - always remember the difference between more or less information and specially between useful verses not useful (every real thing is an information).

Note – All relative are nonsense (don't refer to anything) in the sense of being relative but not all hollow term (bullshit terms) is relative but of course if person try to explained unexplainable obviously, they will just make it relative (still unexplainable but relative bullshit). One more thing to understand that all circular arguments or terms or definitions are relative but all relative is not circular. Though all relative and hollow terms or sentences are meaningless but something can be both together which I call a relative bullshit.

Comparison is not relative bullshit obviously as a retard you can make any thing relative but comparison on the basics of absolute thing about absolute thing which doesn't change that absolute thing just because of comparison is not a relative bullshit.

Chapter 6

Types of People on The Basis of Thoughts

Now you may ask why this chapter exist as if I defined before there can't be different types of thoughts or sub categories or this that relative bullshit and bla bla then how come there is different types of people on the bases of thoughts? Answer to that is quite simple these categories is not about different types of thoughts but is about or on the bases of having thoughts versus not having thoughts or overall rolling delusion or any kind of retardness and overall, how these lead to retardness and progress. These categories are the most important one and any category can be a synonym of these or just combined some of them but no category can take these categories under it in any other way so that these become sub category and there can't be sub category of these because these are on the basis of thoughts and nothing can be without thoughts after all – all of our thinking is just bunch of thoughts. Categories are as follows:

1. Thinker

There is no doubt in that thinkers are not the people who got A grades or understand every thing well or remember every thing or have the most knowledge, thinker are the people who create new thought or new product/invention (for the world) which obviously if not nonsense lead to progress (as some people who are not thinker can claim to be one by creating nonsense). Many people think thinker are the people with high IQ scores but let me tell you IQ test are worthless you can easily find person who has high IQ score but have create nothing, no new thought, no new product/invention, no new theory for progress though it's obvious IQ test work on whether a person understand pattern or not but understanding a pattern in pre existing things and too in thing which doesn't matter never ever will lead a person to create something new and top of all it work on memory a lot - if you give 40-50 IQ test continuously your IQ score will come high at least by 10, that happens because it work on memory how fast a person is capable of memorising pattern in short period of time so he/she can compare it in brain to get result which is again worthless because memory alone has nothing to do with creating new thing even if you search in history no thinker ever born was an so-called memory expert, that's not the only thing most of the best thinker have no degree (which proves person remember the terms/definitions or patterns nothing more than or less than that and it doesn't prove whether that terms/definitions or patterns was real hence progressive or was nonsense and for sure doesn't prove of person being thinker or not) for example Charles Darwin, Michal faraday, John Dalton, James Prescott Joule, Galileo Galilei, Gregor Mendel, Thomas Edison etc. Whole science is on the base of people like these, from which you must understand on your own degree (only of science) is need to know what's known before not to create something new (if you create/connect on your own) and as I told you beforehand what's known beforehand a person can understand on his/her without the of help anybody or even rediscover same knowledge on his/her own (thinker for himself or herself), person become more creative when he/she create things by himself/herself. As I said IQ test are worthless but it's obvious a thinker can easily score at least more than 110 after all it is just a worthless test, after 110 score it doesn't matter whether a person has how much more than that.

But then question arises how to become a thinker? To answer that, first I want you to understand no knowledge can make a person thinker because a person is a thinker or not is shown by what new he/she has created (though having more knowledge gives a scope of being thinker as it give more scope of connecting different stuff hence creating more), if a person creates something on his or her own but it not new for the world then that person can be a thinker because being thinker is absolute and being thinker is just not about one thing but is about thinking to create something new, for world thinker would be the one who created something new according to the world which is absolute too. Though there is no particular way to become thinker but being a absolutist can increase the probability of becoming a thinker (specially for sure would make you able to cope up with the progress) because being a absolutist give you all four qualities which I talked about before hand to understand thing correctly and if you are thinker beforehand then for sure being better absolutist you are going to be better thinker. I want to define absolutism to be absolute so forget any prior meaning of it, absolutism simply means confined to knowledge and information confined by a particular knowledge, any real information (obviously relative or relative bullshit or bullshit is not an something to refer to an information) which can't be confined by a knowledge which obviously is absolute then information can't be considered (considering it is as any thing or anyway for something is a far cry). We will talk about things an absolutist will not do afterward.

No one can become thinker suddenly and no one can just become thinker at any point of there life, there fixed period in which only a person can become thinker after that a person can maintain it till old age, the most important ages is first from birth till seven year of age (if not born unfit) which is obviously when your whole brain structure base system is made to be like an adult brain capabilities, your thinking process is defined and that what decide in what kind of pattern to explore and what you focused on, so if person start thinking of making new things, new thought at or before seven only then for sure that person is a thinker and most probably will remain a thinker till old age, when I say new thing it mean new for that person in the sense that nobody ever told that person how to make that particular thing, after this one may ask why to believe in the significance of early age till 7? Let me tell you the reason -- till the age of seven almost whole brain is developed and that's with a very fast rate, remember I told you brain structure matters and that's obvious, but then what cause only some to become thinker or even cope up with progress? Answer is all of us aren't born as some crazy person who make some crazy nonsense, who make relative bullshit or relative or bullshit, in our early life we explore everything, we question everything and for some we get answers and out of them only some sound reasonable but a person who never get tired of questioning everything and finding answer (really understanding and creating) become thinker and the person who give up become religious become retard, being religious simply mean followings something without questioning it and following something again and again (which obviously not progressive) rather than creating something. Ideally if there is no way a retard get's the benefit of the progress there would be no way people would be becoming retard as either they would get wide out immediately or they would at least be doing (or you can say - be forced to do) minimum something to cope up with the progress.

Second most important age is teenage here again a person has a very great chance to become a thinker because in teenage risk taking factor is one of the highest so that what's makes easy to change your belief system and way of thinking (in the sense breaking your religion, ditching nonsense and learning more knowledge), so teen age is also an great age to become thinker, I hope you would not ask me why teenagers have high risk taking capacity but then also I would tell you –

hormones, though it is not the only reason in teenage, little brain develop is also an reason overall with little less progression, off course not like what happen in childhood but for sure it is the most important stage even if you are already a thinker or normal, after teenage probability of becoming thinker decreased a lot which make harder to change because there is no such special thing except one advantage person's brain don't start loosing plasticity before 25 whether a person is a thinker or not until and unless a person it unfit already, off course if you are thinker you will not lose plasticity fast so basically till 25 still a person have chance to become a thinker after it probability drop down to almost nil specially after 20's it become zero.

If you want to check the history (because you are retards who doesn't understand knowledge just need information) you will see most of the great thinker came up with there great ideas in 20's and sometimes early 30's, though thinker have new ideas throughout in there life till there old age after all that's why they are thinkers but nobody has ever become a thinker in later in his/her life though that's obvious too as I just told you the whole thing, one may argue that this person that person become so-called successful in 40's or so, then let me tell you for sure that person has nothing to do with making new things and for sure that person fall in one of the other category. But I want you to understand history support nothing one should not believe in history and history is worthless except the thought's of thinker and normal at that time because I already told you real progressive thought's are knowledge not just information (in sense of experience too) which would not change with time but history in itself is something which changes with time and have nothing to do with making of any thing new.

So, you should look around see on your own any person who came up with their first new idea must have been young at time who are alive today or right now is somebody came up with a new thought or product/invention must be young right now. Let me tell you one thing in today's world most of the money is managed and influenced and own by young people only who are in there late 20's or early 30's mostly. After all this is the special time form thinkers and others too. One last thing many thinkers' thoughts is always hated (obviously if famous) at least till his/her old age or death by mostly all retards because it is not relative or relative bullshit or bullshit and its obvious in other way too as if something is new which mean a thought of a thinker can opposed by retard people who slow down the progress very significantly. That's why I want most of the people hate this book and dislike this book, because I don't want to talk nonsense and majority is regard. I will make sure that happens. Now if you are retard and under 25 and you accept that and go with the thinking of this book than you can cope of up with progress and if you create something new you can be thinker.

2. Normal

Normal are very important people without them progress is impossible, they are the people who modify the thought or product/invention and theories of thinkers for better progress they not only modify but they also point out fault in particular thinker thoughts or invention and are able to correct them. A person may think normal are not equivalent to thinker or thinker are just better than normal but that's not the reality they also have new thoughts that's why they are able to modify and correct thinker and I told you how every though is result of necessities so it is according to the person - what his/her necessities are, the only difference is thinker start the exploration of purely new field which has lot to explore but then which can't be completed explored without normal.

Same as thinker a person can't become normal at any point of life and nobody can teach a person how to be normal and it is only shown by work whether a person is normal or not. One must remember even though both normal and thinker are on the side of progress that doesn't means that can't clash with each other or clashes can't be in between them but even though that happen it always give rise to more progress after all what is progressive is progressive. But it is important to understand that thinker, normal and defaults also make nonsense but that is never significantly retarding for the field or domain they work in nor that overall make them retarding.

Note – No thinker or normal ever claim to solve people's problem nor claim that you will happy, they just create new or modify things which lead to progress and obviously there claims are for the same which will most probably going make people happy and solve there problems (PS – though it should go without saying there is no nonsensical thing which exist so no new or modification is about that, when I use those terms - new and modification, they are absolutely about what was overall present). One more thing I want to be clear about is use of other terms like genius or something, or people using my terms or categories nonsensically, if you say being genius is being thinker or normal which are category then yes it is a absolute category (this way of categorisation I can use), but if you say being genius is having a certainly level of knowledge then you have to define that certain level absolutely in terms of certain things and if not defined properly it is at least bit relative or if it is defined like having knowledge of 1700's scientists or before then for sure it classify as my definition of retard.

3. Default

I want to define defaults by which I mean people who are progressive for them self by learning thinkers and normal work and copying it (not only menial work) but never create and modify something new so overall they are not exactly progressive for the world but they do maintain the pace of progress and cope up with progress, but obviously this stage can't be there always in most people (it is very volatile stage) as if a person remain default and specially try become better default for long time has a higher change of becoming a thinker or normal (which obviously is dependent on necessities, but that doesn't mean that person will be thinker or normal for world as progress is limited) but obviously a person can become retard also (which mostly the case) or can remain default for all of his/her life which is mostly not the case as people turn to retard obviously because still there are many options to survive as retard.

When we are born, we are default (if not born unfit), we were progressive for our self, for sure we grow and become better mostly at least till 7 but then most people opt to be retard. Defaults are very important for continuation of production of stuff for progress and also for retaining the knowledge, top of all without them there can't be adequate amount for certain stuff for every body who is progressive.

4. Retard

Let's starts with little bit talking about retards. Even talking about them is worthless for any kind of progress, these worthless people are the people who do nothing which lead to progress or cope up with the progress (at least what has been there in last 30-40 years) and that's the most important defining feature. But other than that these people mostly talk about relative or relative bullshit or bullshit things which has no out come, these people are the people who mostly talk about other people instead of thoughts (in the sense of knowledge) because they have nothing of there own and want to create nothing (It is very hard to find something which causes misery just at any level, mostly every with limits makes us happy). Retards are simply the people who doesn't cope up with progress but instead retard it and hence following are there overall most prevailing qualities.

Types of People on The Basis of Thoughts

Retards like more and more relative bullshit or relative or bullshit (as they can't understand it nor anybody can and off course it overall lead to misery) so they doesn't have to think of understanding anything, they are miserable because they have nothing of there own which they have created nor cope up with the progress and chase nonsense and never get that because it don't exist at the first place, they are ignorant (one must remember you can't ignore something if it is not necessary as unnecessary thing don't pop up in anybody's brain, so a ignorant know what he/she is indeed ignoring, off course not exactly as they ignore it just at the moment so they doesn't explore that thing further other than just as an direct reception, this you can call superficial addressing) - there are two way to ignore either you shift the thing after addressing that so you doesn't have ignore it again hence permanent ignorance or you just doesn't shift it may be because you can't and keep on ignoring while addressing it superficially, they cry a lot but they simile a lot too sometimes - for the same reason that they are miserable and they have nothing to do, so to divert other people attention and their own attention they cry, simile and specially they simile when they are nervous and being nervous is nothing more than not having thoughts and then things to do which they don't have before hand as they just have delusion of having thoughts so basically they can only talk nonsense mostly [and off course there is no relation in between smiling and happiness, and smiling is not a good thing or the bad thing it is just only thing you can do when you try to use maximum muscles of your face that's why people smile(not retards) when they have lot of stimulation to show that they have lot of stimulation and also to have more stimulation which is not necessary thing to do (there is no doubt in that)- it quiet obvious there are nonsense out there like if you smile you will be healthy], they are highly biased, they are coward as they don't have any of there own thought and there is an old saying 'coward are bold in crowd and weak man become murderer in mob' there is no doubt in that all the people who do protest (specially destroying things) and these kind of things there are retard and even you can check this also by stopping person out from a mob or from a protest and ask him/her why are you doing and why are you doing this and you will get mostly one kind of answers these people are bad that people are bad we didn't got what should be getting, new laws should be made or some kind of law should be removed nothing more than that and they have nothing to do with progress nor they can think of progress nor can create new thought or product/invention.

For example, let say there is group of people who are doing protest against air pollution you stop one of them and ask what air pollution is? You will get the same answers which I just told and after that most probably that person going to say co2 is more, ask that person how much more that compared to starting to earth or all period of earth or for human or plant to be problematic? Off course they doesn't know that (most probably doesn't even know the biggest reservoir of co2 and what it is exactly), how come he/she can know anything who is just protesting instead of considering things and working on it (obviously you can't work on something if you really doesn't know a single thing about that thing or anything other then term which hollow for you even if it really mean something if you consider nothing really), than ask what are the type of plant? (c3, c4), how much concentration they need for there best efficiency? Again he/she will not have answer, then ask for- do he/she know what Scrubber, Arrester and how they work? Most probably they will here this word first time in there life from your mouth and forget about knowing how they work, then ask him/her do they have something better technology or better something which will be helpful? Off course he/she will be having nothing the only thing he/she will be wanting is to stop this or that (mostly its all about envy, jealousy, wanting more stuff, taking nonsense and retarding the progress). Most importantly ask a person how we define a pollutant or toxin? Obviously, it is defined by limits and for something (Comparatively).

Let that an analogy of the above example (scenario) let say there is an engine when it start working it got heated up now it efficiency is going down now what to do? stop that engine? off course not, a thinker and normal will try to find ways to cool it down so that they can fetch maximum result and progress without stopping but for retard first they can't create engine at the first place on there own and second only solution they know is either stop something or create some kind of a law nothing more than that, either they support something or oppose something, either they believe or don't believe but they don't prove anything or create/modify any new thought or product (and obviously they don't cope up with progress but yet want benefits of it) and there is no doubt in that if a person create something useful whether it reduce pollution or something else people will buy that thing from them but then that is far beyond retard comprehension (and definitely I am not calling co2 an pollutant nor I am talking about idiotic carbon capture plants).

Now let me tell you a simple information retard burn more money in advertising about environment which they call making people concern about environment or aware of environment than taking any kind of progressive action and let me tell you another fact you will see people here and there taking about global warming and all or other thing they don't understand even a bit about, let me tell you there is no problem because of global warming and earth is not hotter than ever (and we are thermos regulators and there would no problem because of warming in any way ever which will cause problem for progressive people or something as a doom of our species if we use all the oil in within 5 decades), the people who talk about so called more co2 in environment or more warmer earth they compare it with pre industrialisation (basically what was at early 1700's generally) not with early earth, instead of that according to every estimate earth must have more concentration of gas to have more warming effect in early earth (than what it is today with more green house gases) because of different reasons (and for sure our species have see more warmer temperature than this with lot more fluctuation), most important result of that is it supported life and top of all earth is more warmer than ever or it's just more warm is nothing more than a shitty concept as earth must have been more warmer (term is purely relative when retards use that) and for the retards who don't known about the primitive earth and doesn't read standard book which they can't as they are retard, don't forget life evolve when there was no oxygen and then organism created this oxygenating environment from reducing environment (and that's one of reason why life can't evolve again) and retard don't know even know at want concentration of co2 which type of plant work the best and top of all so called problem of heating (if ever that would really be a problem) can be easily solved if people think of doing something to aerosol of stratosphere (defiantly reducing co2 is so idiotic statement anyway) but right now we have no problem because of heating and retards like fooling around and saying stop this or that (especially at end they say give us more things).

If we talk about people cut tree so they should be stopped or something then let me tell you nobody do unnecessary thing if you create something which fulfil same necessities why would a person will do that (by the way plating millions of small tree of a feet or so is just worthless comparatively in name of high co^2, quiet frankly trying to plant big tress like 10feet or so would be more crazy wastage of money) and most important thing all problem arise because retard exist, when retard will be whipped out all the problem will be solved on there own for most part (for example we don't have to use more fossil fuel to do more progress we can simply cut supply to retards and patch up the leaks, basically we can even use less and do more progress). The only thing a retard can do to maintain progress whether that retard is concerned about climate or whatever is he/she should kill himself/herself.

Now Continuing with most common properties of retard, they are kids of witch (witch or witch magic is term to refer to all hollow terms which people mostly use) as they talk about magic but them self can't do anything or can't perform any magic (basically really doing stuff), seems like there witch mother taught them what shit to vomit from there mouth but forget to tell not vomit it everywhere. Retard people don't have any of there own thought they may think they have which is going to be nonsense only which is not real nor a real thought for something which I already explained you why. But the most retarding thing is that they are always has more in number and percentage through out the history and today also but then this is the last century for them because they have crossed all limit of retardness (especially we are very close to ultimate progress at least quality wise) and shown how unfit they are to survive they are fat and dumb they make up to 85% of today's population and how I conclude that? I conclude that on the basis that 85% of the world population has no record of any kind of success or coping up the progress at all.

One best example to see these retards thinking is through social media it is well known that social media create mental and physical illness and even necrosis as you are not really using your brain and body to be progressive instead you are retarding if you are using that, off course it create all these problem in retard only because they are the only people who try to make thing nonsense because they don't have any of there own thing or thought to work on but the funny part is even they know it create that kind of problem still they use social media after all they like nonsense because they have nothing else to do, though there is no doubt in that social media is just worthless and some people think it is for business (not of nonsense) what a joke if that going to be the reality all the retards must be producing something and be doing business, the social media which claim there these many people connect to create thing who use there app then ask a question out of how many people and what you consider as an useful product? Overall internet is useful to bit transfer information but then question is what information and whether it is knowledge or not (one of the most important thing is not only most of the internet/media content and connections retard the progress but there very existence and there maintenance is just crazy retardness, it's very important for progress that we should reduce the size of current media and internet to less than 1% of it's current size within a decade). PS – I do know there will be lot's of idiot who would be like look internet increased the speed of communication so much that's why it is so important, I can understand for an instance if somebody say's telegraph increased the speed of communisation for use by 1000 times but I can understand if somebody say internet increased it even by twice, other famous nonsense can be it is progressive to just watch people doing something or just to listen nonsense.

Just to give an example of geniuses of retards according to them is one day social media will be progress, filled with knowledge and not filled with misinformation or basically relative bullshit or relative or direct bullshit and overall will lead to progress. Obviously, something like that we never happen and social media would not exist till the end of this century because of very simple reasons. First - we don't need it for progress in any way because we already have things which are filled with knowledge and not nonsense which are known as science books which lead to progress (though most of book on the name of science are written by renovated retards and are obviously retarding). Second – there is no such thing like explaining the same knowledge in different way or explaining it better nor there is such like a person have knowledge but can't fetch information from it that's why need other people, hence it is total nonsense that different or more people are needed for leading progress. Third - it didn't facilitate transfer of information nor ever be will able to do that as internet does facilitate transfer of information but there is no need of social media – especially internet is not the cause of creation of more knowledge nor making people more knowledge which mostly is attributed to internet as without that also we were transferring information confined by knowledge and knowledge (books are still the only source of knowledge and information confined by knowledge and direct physical books and notebooks will never be outclassed by anything, if you don't understand that - just stop reading) instead of that internet has caused the biggest retardness then ever because of facilitating nonsense. Fourth – most of the population is retard and that's why social media exist at the first and because that's the case then people will be searching of retardness only and better algorithm help you to find what you are searching for thus making retards more retard. Fifth - especially there is not such thing like interacting with lot of people while really knowing them as we can't know even hundreds of people properly.

Anyway if retard population will not be there for sure the technology we have today can be there 20 century ago or who knows how many years before people would have what we have today and what else we would be having today (exactly), there is no doubt these retard are always there in the way of progress even though progress give comfort to all and even when some thing can save there life still they will in the way of that progress for example in old time there was an person known as 'Galen of Pergamon' that person is not allowed to do dissection on human and you must be knowing why because it was illegal back then because of retard people concept of god and ghost etc. (There are still so many laws which are retarding to that significance) because of which progress not only stopped but also created myths, though Galen was a great thinker (his work include development in understanding circulatory system, respiratory system, nervous system, larynx, sex organ and spinal cord etc.) but off course doesn't matter how great thinker you are without proper tools and proper observation a person always create mess and nonsense, he dissected animals to understand anatomy of human which give rise more myths like body and brain (problem) are same - there is no difference, human physiology and anatomy is like other animal and can be treated in same way and lead to continuity of some old myth at time like men has more rids than women and men has more teeth than women now off course the myth of more teeth is so absurd but as I told you most of population is always have been retard and all thinker and normal don't work on the same thing so until Andreas Vesalius came in who told teeth are equal in both male and female and he himself said this 'Aristotle and many others say men have more teeth than women; it is no harder for anyone to test this than it is for me to say it is false, since no one is prevented from counting teeth' but then you can understand retard people even can't count teeth on there own.

If you think people are not that retard today then you are in delusion for example there are more myth than ever about penis, vagina, hymen and so other human body part off course in between retards only because as per the real biology we have done very big progress in last 100 years to achieve or create core biology, still retard people use word without putting any brain - keep thinking they understand something, one example is that when they use word heart while describing thoughts as retard never think twice even why to use that word at the first place, let me tell you the word heart was used in the old time while describing the thoughts because Galen and some other people use to believe thoughts also(this is important as also some how become absolute for some very particular thoughts – of course I don't how) come from heart and there is something like hope inside heart, off course Andreas Vesalius proved that is just another myth but this myth was created because first people can't dissect human back then and specially people came up with this mentality I think because first - it is relative bullshit so great reasoning for majority, second - when person die only two thing just any person can notice superficially and easily that lungs is not working and heart is not pumping so people connect no thought to death of heart hope or something like that (as they simple doesn't understand cells obviously and there death), off course they didn't connected it with lungs because before 1700 there were no real chemistry and oxygen was discovered at 1774 by Joseph Priestle and also by Antoine Lavoisie independently (and Galen was the first person to really define that arteries carry blood which carry oxygen obviously while not really explaining oxygen and also differentiating veins), so that people can really understand air and why no real chemistry before 1700s? Answer is very simple because retard believe in nonsense magic and alchemy so they just retard things and spread nonsense while opposing any real progress. Just one more point most probably traditional double-lobed heart symbol is inspired by the shape of the human female buttock as they appear from behind, whatsoever the case is we just doesn't think of unreal thing nor make unreal thing and if you understood nonsense as explained by me then, I think till now you would clear about above stuff.

So there is no doubt in that people have become more retard then ever (not at all coping up with the progress) and crossed all limit (lot of idiot today are way more idiot then idiots of century ago, which mean more in number of more idiot people then ever before), off course there is no doubt in that most (at least 99%) of the information in internet is nonsense which means it is not at information at all in any sense of being useful specially for reference and most of population use internet for nonsense only which you must have understood till now how retarding it is and that's why nonsense thing dominate at internet and though earth hasn't change in it's nature(content of earth- really) it is as it was and there is no doubt in that technology we have seen in last 250 years can be there lot before than that, still I think if you are thinker or normal you will enjoy the best show in the history of this world the 'doom of retards' I can't think something better than this can happen in sense of directly maintenance of progress.

At last I would like to talk about two more qualities of retard first they are optimistic or pessimistic because of nonsense reason which mean they are optimistic or pessimistic for no real reason (in which they think they are going to better off or more miserable because of so and so or if so and so is not done) and being optimistic or pessimistic nothing more than retardness and doesn't refer to anything other than being delusional, second they talk about passion and they call them self passionate let me tell you no thinker ever have being present who was passionate about any thing though it is obvious because passionate about some thing (if we try to define it) is being biased and not creating new thoughts and things, being passionate is being an sticking nothing more than that. One last thing I don't who is going to read this book because I can't stop retards to read this book nor I want to do that but remember one thing any retard can read and remember thing (specially just terminologies without really understanding or just memorizing any hollow terminologies) but retards can't be more creative to cope up with progress and be progressive.

5. Renovated Retard

As the name suggest these people are retard and have all the qualities of retards but with little bit of modification, just like retards they have none of there own thought to cope up with the progress and get benefits of the progress, but the four modification they have are

1. They are recessive pseudo-dominant by this I mean first they doesn't express anything because they doesn't have anything but then they expresses things which nothing more than relative bullshit or relative or bullshit as they still doesn't have anything, so whatsoever thing (allegedly) they start talking about- more and more the popularity they gain (as retard are more in number who follow them who think they know/understand something nonsensical i.e. being delusional) they become more and more pseudo dominant (delusion of expressing something, but definitely doing certain thing afterwards which are very retarding and promoting them or simply asking for more things) about or for that thing even that much they start thinking that they are better than normal and even sometimes they think they are better than thinkers, so basically they move from recessive to pseudo dominant on particular topic and change there own thing into more bigger bullshit or relative or relative bullshit by using retards (depending upon popularity), off course on the same topic (or maybe deferent nonsensically) because topic is bullshit or relative or relative bullshit so it can go big or small, after all they are nonsense but don't forget they look dominant only in the so-called eyes of retards but in reality (the only possibilities) they are still coward and have no real thing to express.

2. They use the concept of more this is the most important part, whatsoever relative or relative bullshit thing they talk on they split into more and more parts which are also relative in itself (at least) or they copy one part of relative thing and just increase it in number which is also relative in itself as they are derived from relative thing only or they directly add bullshit, and doing this don't take effort because they don't make any thing new they just had something purely worthless (nonsensical) and split it or increase the number of something which doesn't exist (most popularly language systems which doesn't refer to anything) so there is nothing to really compare from or to think on so they just say any

terminology and under which they put particular situation or example the same way they give birth to relative or relative bullshit so basically it an unlimited retardness and can go on forever.

For example if they say good they going to tell 20 types of good or this this become ultimate good when done again and again, if they say great they going to say 50 type of great, if they say sin they going to say 100 type or doing same thing more and more time make some kind of difference or more of same thing make any difference categorically, if they going to say of rule of some thing they going to say 20, 40 ,100.. rules as many as they want as there is no comparison can be made in any of the above systems and they can go as many types of any thing as they want. Another way of using of concept of more is the more frequency of a particular word, in this case even though retard doesn't understand a word but because of hearing again and again same word they come in the delusion of understanding it (this mostly the way because of which retards can't even identify direct bullshit).

Remember retards like more and more relative or relative bullshit or direct bullshit as they can't understand it nor anybody can (but off course its overall lead to misery), so they don't have to think of understanding anything. One thing which is quite obvious more the relative bullshit or relative you try to connect with more information then bigger it becomes. A crazy famous renovated retard would try to talk about every thing (allegedly) and the only reason retards think they can is just that they can talk nonsense on every thing which anyone can do and it is limitless as it is meaningless.

3. They make 'relative or relative bullshit' relative with each other or to other, so again no limit of nonsense for example they going to say this is good at so and so condition but at so and so condition this is not good (which doesn't necessarily mean it is bad even though that what relative bullshit allegedly means) or after this only it will be good or bad or other relative bullshit or simply saying a category creates some sort of limit (relative bullshit), so you can understand using these three things situationally and simultaneously, they make a big pile of nonsense. This particular thing is very important for creating laws, rules etc. and getting lots of benefit out of them.

4. They claim to solve problem which doesn't exist by solution which doesn't exist, they give solution which doesn't exist or is not a solution for problem which they don't understand hence because of those things they tell people relative

bullshit or bullshit or relative because of which people (retards) and they all together do things which are crazy retarding, and meanwhile renovated retards gets lot of benefits of the progress which they never did or cope up with instead of that they retard it like crazy.

Even though I covered all qualities of renovated retard still I will give name of the stream which is for sure purely for renovated retards, for the people who are under 30 and specially under 25 and want to change to thinker or normal or defaults, they should not even listen to these people even for proving that they are nothing more than retards. Major streams are as follows

1. Teachers and Coaches

First let me tell you thinkers and normal never teach they just create thing or write books and even somehow they use to teach they only teach there own thing and have mentality that they can't make any body a thinker, they can just teach what they have created and even if somehow because of some reason which is very rare that they teach something of others, if they do so they are horrible at teaching that (because of unwillingness they use skipping) and for all this I just said you can check history if you want to, you may ask what's the reason? The reason is very simple, first- they want to create more new thoughts and things so they just can't teach the same thing again and again, second - they known a progressive person will seek for progressive thing and will read/explore there work and will be able to understand on his/her own, third – easy publishing of books. Now let me tell you why teachers are so retard, first almost 90% teachers think they teaches better than other which mean they think there is no need of improvement if possible and they keep on teaching the same thing in the same way every single year which nor they understand nor they created.

There are two fields in which teacher teaches, first the non sense one which just consist of renovated retards and second is science in which most of the teachers are renovates retard (at least today), problem with these are they don't teach something of there own as they have created nothing, they teaches other people thing in this scenario one can't say how much they understand by that particular thing and even they are teaching (just repeating term written in the progressive books) what exactly it is or not and how it will lead progress they just doesn't know (PS – if a person which is just a teacher writes a book on a subject and there is already an standard book for that subject then the problem with that is, the teacher's book can't lead progress but definitely can retard progress and I have no idea why a person who have nothing new – absolute to say why that person should write a book?) . Though generally these people make thought of thinker and normal relative at least or exploit it if was bit relative or nonsense any way or mould it into nonsense if was not nonsenses before (obviously shows there retardness). At maximum the people who teaches science can be lower end of defaults so this is only category of teaching can have exception otherwise all teachers or any other profession mentioned below are renovated retards. Generally better or best default (people who have lot of knowledge of different field and domain) don't even teach, writing is a far cry, that's why most of the written work is nonsense and there is generally not too much in between today. But I don't understand what's the need of teacher if you know how to read and write, then why you wouldn't directly read the standard book written by thinker or normal or may be by better defaults which has become standard.

Most important thing one must understand there is no such person like a very impressive teacher or very correctly or better teaching teacher for something, first - I don't know why they exist because if thinker or normal has written a book (which a theory or explanation of a product) or created something then why people need another person to explain that thing, the reality is there – there is no need of teachers that's why most of the thinker and normal ever born really don't have been teacher and even though if they have a teacher they do different thing and create different thing than there teacher has taught them that's why they are thinker or normal. Second - according to retards the better or best teacher is the one who demonstrate, it is very obvious demonstration proves nothing (considering people think they can understand relative or relative bullshit), specially experiments are there to create things, if a person tells you it is just an experiment which doesn't create anything it is nothing more than waste of money (most probably crazy relative and relative bullshit they are talking about) and top of for particular demonstration what reasoning a person give is also something to think on because retard don't have the prior knowledge and most probably either they don't want to understand or can understand some knowledge, so they accept any reasoning for any demonstration, let me tell you why retard think demonstration add any value, they think so because generally it is easy remember visuals then words as it's about which stimulate the brain more and specially if they learned (which is basically a delusion of retard they understand any thing for most part) through word before hand then visuals are shown or both together then they just memorize better but off course they never really led to progress so basically it help them to be a memory expert (specially of terms) nothing more than that, they really don't understand anything nor they create anything new or modify anything. Remember there is no such thing like an abridge of a useful progressive thing nor there is a such thing like explaining a particular knowledge in better way either you explain it or you don't.

I think there is no need to talk too much why all coach are renovated retards as first- there is no such thinking like changing knowledge just because somebody is personally teaching you that and if you have knowledge you call always fetch information from that on yourself, second - even a default would not be a coach because obviously it is just would be retarding to that default who do cope up with the progress, third – again there is no such thing like explaining the same knowledge in different way, fourth – the claims of coaches to make people successful (if it means progressive in any other way then what they would be any way learning that thing or especially clamming to make people thinker or normal) is obviously idiotic (nonsense).

If you wonder how to find a real thinker or normal not just a default (teacher) to work with then it is very easy first they must have created something new or must have modified something. Look there is no secret of progress because if there is something progressive then that thing has to be there by which I mean not a secret or witch magic or holy moly magic or whatever so don't let anybody tell you there is a secret of progress or progress is a secret. Particular information makes something particular, any relative bullshit or relative on information can't lead to progress, so if you want to do particular thing for progress then you need particular information (mostly just knowledge directly) not relative bullshit or relative. At the end I want to tell you the 5 biggest, funniest nonsense which renovated retards teach. Order is as follows

1. How to teach or learn, or how to create new or modify something.
2. What exactly to do for any scenario (which is generalization of scenarios which is relative bullshit or relative in itself and then solution is relative bullshit).
3. How to wear a condom, insertion of menstrual cup, tampon etc. (from props to human being) and how to fuck (or even you should fuck or not).
4. Exercises (how to do this or that and what to do for this or that like you have a muscle which exist for doing nothing or you just don't use it or if you did you are doomed).
5. What to eat (just like you can't eat every thing without repeating frequently if you are fit to be healthy) or how much you should eat in general or of anything particular (if you are fit).

Types of People on The Basis of Thoughts

If you need or you have any person to teach you the above things then I may want to teach you how tie a knot on neck (of course you don't know that beforehand). Take a rope create two bends and then take one end rap it around the bends 3-4 times then takes that end pass it through the rare loop then hold the knot while pulling on the noose loop to tighten the knot.

2. Memory or Brain Expert

As I already told you more memory is just not the alone thing which makes you creative to create more thing, now a days there are lot of memory expert who have created nothing and talk about how to memorise this or that, I want to say just one thing if something is really necessary to remember according to you specially knowledge and information confined by knowledge, you will remember it and top of all if you create something you will remember it at any cost quiet frankly till you death doesn't matter how much of brain degradation you suffer from in itself (remember in any kind of amnesia it's almost nil probability you will forget knowledge and very low probability you will forget information confined by knowledge, mostly what get lost is just information and relative or relative bullshit or direct bullshit - mostly of language system).

One thing which memory expert think is that practice make person achieve thing, I have heard so many times for confidence or for whatever do practice, practice and practice, if you believe so you are retard, practice is for retard or to develop a reflex. If person have low self esteem, self confidence, self worth that simply means that person have nothing of his/her own nor knowledge to cope up with progress and seek for practice, even renovated retard have delusion of having little bit self worth which comes from popularity of renovated retards but off course they don't create anything they just fool around. I think these retards have forget brain is not something which store and then vomit occasionally instead of that brain is something which should be working at every moment and any place it is capable of thinking new thing but off course not the same case for retards (especially unfit).

Another expert which people can claim to be is brain experts, they are going to tell you how to grow brain and become genius. To that kind of bullshit or relative bullshit, I just want to say growing brain doesn't make you a genius as genius people are the people who are genius because they did a particular thing and their brain did particular thing not general bla bla bla, other than that something can't happen for nothing or there can't be something for nothing by which I mean your brain just can't grow and grow just because it has more supplements or because of other relative or relative bullshit as it has to be there for something. Hence so-called brain and memory experts are nothing more than renovated retards who talk nonsense here and there (no wonder why they are becoming increasing famous). Quiet frankly if you are looking for brain or memory expert you are running away from knowledge and want to believe that you are useful and got some knowledge, by the way that's an delusion. Now a days there so-called of experts of just anything who have no knowledge what so ever to cope up with the progress.

3. Sportsperson, Bodybuilder, etc.

First let me tell you it is very easy to focus on something which predominantly physical because in this process person don't use too much brain more or less as they use reflexes and do the same thing again and again which nothing more than retardness. Obviously, there is a point till your muscles can grow but not more and more forever at least that you understand whether you understand muscles or myofibrils in particular or not hence lead to retardness. There is no doubt in that these people don't add any values to any thing and has nothing to do with progress and there is no doubt in that playing is not something harmful and playing doesn't makes a person retard but playing/doing the same thing again and again or watching another person playing and saying this is my team/person is nothing more than retardness and if we talk bodybuilding and all it is retarding a person should be fit not a bodybuilder big jumbo dumb ass and there is no doubt in that being a bodybuilder has no advantage nor a bodybuilder live longer or more healthier than just fit person or something else instead of that being a bodybuilder can have very harmful effect over long period of time i.e. being less fit or eventually becoming unfit. One thing just in case you don't understand (as you are a retard) on you own yet that you don't have to learn exercises from anybody else and if you have a muscle for sure you use it (there can't be something for nothing).

4. Leaders, so-called son of gods/lesser god or whatever

Leaders are worthless, renovated retards nothing more than that (always), if you wonder how leader gain power and popularity then let tell you one single quality of there which is clarity in the sense of repeating and straight forward creating relative or relative bullshit or direct bullshit, clarity to retard make them think to trust person and clarity for retards means nothing more than no but, no if, no why, no how just speak relative bullshit or relative or bullshit and tell them what to do and again remember retard like nonsense because they can't understand it so they doesn't have to understand any thing nor they want to, at best they just want to have thing (especially more and more). But you can understand this all above things thinkers and normal would not like to do that's why thinker and normal never become leader or want to become leader and they just can't talk relative or relative bullshit or direct bullshit all day and they want to do progress because of which doesn't think nonsense for those field or stuff they just think realistic as you can say and of course they think when they think (when they do progress) not in the delusion i.e., thinking they can think when they can't think.

Let us consider the progress of last two centuries what you think it was depended on Ghandi, Karl mark, Hitler, and others whatever god or whatever witch magic or holy moly magic? off course not, it was depend on people like James Watt, Michal Faraday, Gregor Medal, John Dalton, Thomas Edison, Nicola tesla, etc. Whatsoever technology and thoughts you see today is all covered by these kind of people more or less and still there work influence on us and contribution is incomparable and just for the information retards who belief politics topic or basically topic is influenced by retards like Ghandi, Mark, gods etc. then the answer is no the topics are influenced by people of science as because of there thoughts only today in politics shitty religion (especially of holy moly) is not the only topic (just to say) though still it is the most important topic in politics but yes if progress is there in any way it is because of thinker or normal not because of leader or gods or lesser gods or whatever relative bullshit or bullshit.

If we talk about so called lesser god and son of gods they are also worthless they also haven't created anything (irrespective of the thing or people they try to refer to or they just don't as we know major thinker and normal who created the major things very clearly), except they do create big pile of nonsense which is mythology as I told you what renovated retard use you can easily see all this in mythologies, you can easily see mythologies exactly tell what to do because retards don't have brain to do progress and they want someone to tell them where, how and what to do (obviously not some progressive things) and how to create a big pile of nonsense and what a joke that is so called god created every thing (relative bullshit or bullshit) and they or there so called sons yet created didn't except nonsense (though that make sense) which has nothing to do with progress instead of that it retard progress, off course just what retard are and that's what retards do. Why history mostly so worthless? off course because it is full of these leaders, so-called called son of god, bullshit or relative bullshit, show of power of controlling retard going from one of them to another. If you follow a leader, you are a retard (most probably one of the worst idiots).

One quiet obvious thing is if a person didn't create anything, modified anything and still famous then for sure that person is a renovated retard. Being famous is nothing more than most of the people thinking they know you or any particular thing and obviously most of the people want to know relative bullshit or relative or bullshit as it is meaningless so that that they don't have burden of doing thing or thinking about things and can fool around - wherever they want to, but yet they want everything or most of the things even though they retard progress and who so ever agree with this or that retardness i.e., renovated retard they become famous.

5. Journalist

First, I want to tell you something if nonsense and worthless information is one big pile of nonsense you can always find most of it through journalist and if knowledge is something collectively you can't find any of it through journalist. Journalist have no brain for progress and has nothing to do with knowledge nor they ever create something, they are completely worthless for any progress. At best journalist know how to read and write properly. Do you know how journalism start? Even you don't, you can easily guess when retards try to be in between every thing and they worked like spy and then they started talking nonsense in public, still it is the same, they can never create anything of there own which can be useful or talking something useful. Journalist are the renovated retard who make retards delusional about understanding a relative bullshit or relative or direct bullshit (it is mostly done by journalism) specially on the bases of using it again and again. If retard heard a term many time, he/she just assume they understand it and don't forget retards are very biased.

I just want to ask you, how somebody who didn't created anything, modified anything, does cope up with any kind of progress but yet can talk about everything (real, obviously allegedly) and is the person who wanted to address more and more people who are retard then how would that person would talk about progress not retardness?

Types of People on The Basis of Thoughts

6. Just writers/so-called content creators (now a days)

Thinkers and normal are not writers/content creators they only write to share the thing which they have found on there own so that it can lead to progress. But most of books are written by just writers who haven't created anything and they don't have anything of there own (useful as obviously you can have you own relative bullshit or relative or direct bullshit which has nothing to do with anything). If a person had written or created content even a single just history book or book/content on other people/products or book on those thoughts of thinker/normal for sure that person is a renovated retard nothing more than that. The person who dwells in past for sure have nothing to do in present. Other renovated retard are the people who write inspirational or motivational book they are also retard and have created nothing, inspiration is something all retards want because it is relative they easy consider (delusion) somebody else achievement as there own and start relating a person with them self (which is an delusion that as they think they can do that) and motivation is one of the biggest relative bullshit, how come a general statement can make or change person particular necessities and even if do so how a sudden change in necessity can create an necessity which last long, answer is off course not it can't that why it is relative bullshit and if you really want motivation then just gather any nonsense because it is nothing more than that.

Now let me tell you another nonsense which new comparable to all other nonsense which is self help and personal development, let me tell you there is no such thing like that (the terms-obviously they doesn't mean anything) there hype started after 1950 and even the word personal development don't exist really before 1900's and again 1950 is important because after this retard crossed all limit of retardness (the difference between progressive people and retards are bigger than ever) we will talk more about that later. Now you can understand why every single renovated retard talk about personal development today because it is relative bullshit which has no limit.

Another thing you will find renovated retard telling about is this or that is the way to communicate and learn communication skill, let me tell these all thing are for retards, If you want to learn communication skills that simply means you don't have any of your own thought (not necessarily being a thinker or normal) to talk on because no one can explain a way to explain your own thought better then what you yourself can (and what is absolute it is explained in absolutely exactly same way) and there is no such thing like public speaking skills it is nothing more than talking nonsense because most of the people are retards.

Now if you believe in self help and personal development then let me tell you self help kind of thing are need by the people who are retard, if after using that kind of relative bullshit and you claim to be changed by them it doesn't mean more than that and can't mean more than that – that you were a retard and you are still a retard who is trying to be crazy ignorant or delusional to reduce misery at certain instance (and you know what? It can work but overall it will cause more misery and another thing which can be possible for another scenario is just not trying to be more retards (most probably only rate is reduced) but being more delusional or ignorance is not becoming less retard so definitely this is not the case for self help nonsenses (because it is nonsense). And remember because not doing something any more just doesn't undo things and will not change you into thinker or normal or default (though retard do more retarding stuff and self help is more relative bullshit only) for example if retard standing on the dick of another retard and he broke it even he doesn't stand on his dick anymore doesn't mean his dick is repaired, it will not going to change the fact that retard is a men with a broken dick and doing more retarding things will certainly not going to repair the unrepairable (though because of all that I don't wonder why contradictory statement which are obviously relative or relative bullshit are famous, like it's never too late, ever body got this or that potential always, everybody is born with something unique, people are different - born to do different, anybody can do anything, you have knowledge but you just can't apply it, you know stuff but you don't understand it etc.

Note - You become thinker/normal only if you create new or modify things and default only if you cope of any particular progress at least.

Now other type of nonsense writers who are purely the kids of witch who talk some kind of magic, one of there famous magic is what you think that will when, say positive so that positive will happen, first - there is no such think like positive, second - if we talk about that what you will think will happen just because you think something particular then let me tell it means logically that there is something other than three things which I told you on which necessity depend and that same thing comes under necessity and take necessity inside simultaneously and thing doesn't get over there, to understand overall take that this way let say you have to draw or imagine a graph in which red circle representing thing on which necessities depends and blue circle which define necessities, can blue circle be inside and outside of red circle simultaneously in that graph? Can both circles be equal? Can both circles can produce equal or reciprocal results? of course not and remember what you can't create, you can't think of at the first place as obviously you really can't think unreal (nonsense). Now you can understand it just doesn't make any sense.

I don't have any advice for you as advices are for retards only as progress is done by knowledge and information confined by knowledge. If you take any even by a thinker or normal instead of renovated retard and retard then also I want you tell you one simple thing need of advices (how to do something) is only there when you are not sure why you want to something and what you want to do (knowledge is not just how to do something) for example if a chair is in between you and an body you are looking to then for sure you know why you want to move the chair and you are sure you want to move chair then for sure you know how to do it as you will know how much you want to move and where you want to move, there is no but's and if's involved in between nor there is an need of any advice. For instance, somebody give an advice in this scenario first that person is a renovated retard imposing his/her things (mostly probably dome of the worst nonsense) on you and then even if you follow that then it simply means you are a retard as if you are going to be thinker/normal you are going to be because you did something on your own because of your own and default when you cope up with the progress not nonsense or do retarding things. So, the only thing I want to say as I don't have any advice for you, just do whatsoever you want to do (real), just do it.

7. So-called artist

All artist is mostly nothing more than renovated retard and have nothing to do with progress and there are only two thing which led to progress and put under art. First is painting/drawing, if person paint/draw it boost imagination and push person to create new thing (thinker create new thing through drawing they just don't copy something, just like prior pioneer architects) but a real thinker and normal can't be just a painter/drawer (for example better architects applied basic physics and mathematics to create better) and would never consider painting as his/her main stream for that you can check history too. Second is music off course not music which include vocal or retard singer, I am talking about the music which don't include any kind of vocal in any form, thinker and normal can be musicians or can like that kind of music (as it can help them to create new sound which boost there thinking of creating new things, though that's not important anymore as we have perfect best language with us i.e. English) and every particular sound is music and certainly everybody is not deaf, still they will not consider that as there main stream as it is very menial, for this also you can check history if you want to. Now let me tell you who are purely renovated retard dancers, actors, singer, so called literature writer and specially poets, other kind of musician, etc.

Only retard like these kind of people because they create pseudo experience (experience not create by oneself and which lead to delusions) or in other word they make lot of nonsense in between, one must remember there is no such thing like pseudo necessities (and pseudo experience is something unreal) for example if a person watch, read, listen so-called romantic fiction that simply means that person lack romance in life that's why to fulfil that necessity he/she watch, listen, read that and off course create pseudo experience (which at least means people thinking something has to do something with them even though it has nothing to do with) which will not last long as it was nothing more than delusion (you can think that you can think about something or particular relative bullshit or relative even though you can't, but obviously delusion doesn't make you happy overall instead of that lead to more misery), if person don't lack romance he/she will not watch, listen, read that kind of things as thought of lacking will never pop in his/her mind nor does the thought of watching, reading, listening that kind of thing will never pop up in there brain as it will be unnecessary to have a thought like that, that's why thinker and normal don't watch, read, listen, write any kind of so-called fiction, only retard and renovated retards do that as they are retards.

Arts is the biggest scam market today in which most popular and biggest scams are paintings, ancient collectable, clothes, hype of anything and calling it arts or genius arts to say it is something useful, progressive or special.

Author's Note – After reading all this, if you are above 30 and you are retard and you accept it then I will suggest you to become a renovated retard because you will not able change for sure into thinker or normal as you have a degrading brain, degrading body, memory full of nonsense, retardness around you and you roll in it, thus even going into default is tough too (most probably there is no way) because there would no witch magic going to happen and nor anybody in the history is there who become thinker or normal suddenly after 30 with no prior record of the thinking of thinker and normal nor it is logically possible (and obviously it's all relative or relative bullshit like it's never too late, every body got the potential, be optimistic, you are going to get what you are destine for etc.), and let me tell you it has lot of profit, first - it is very easy, you don't have to use your brain more really to create more non sense, second - you will accumulate lot of wealth by doing and specially talking nonsense and selling it. I want you to be so because more the number renovated retard increase more it make the doom of retard fun, faster and we don't need more defaults for most part (and obviously we overpopulated), and remember don't think anybody would think any thing about you in particular as they can't (just they can be in delusion of thinking in particular) because obviously there is just nonsense you are going to talk nor they will point you out as they can't (exactly, though can differentiate superficially which will be very useful for you as they want to roll in more nonsense) because retards can't do that on there own and thinker and normal don't care mostly (mostly showing there retardness of ignorance, until and unless you directly try to do something for there stuff) and also they know thinker, normal and default search for progressive thing to be progressive, retards will search for nonsense and renovated retard. So overall by increasing renovated retards and cutting fund going to retards and any retarding systems is the best fun quick indirect way to cut lose retards and there retardness.

One thing to always remember why retards opt for crazy retardness when there is no way or way back anyway not only because there is no way back (i.e. they already have a degrading brain, degrading body, memory full of nonsense, retardness around them and they roll in it) but also because especially relative bullshit is 'relative bullshit' so it can be taken in any way and specially when they try to ignore that there is no way they are going to be progressive, but obviously it creates more retardness and make them more retard, I am not saying a retard who can't change can become progressive but at least rolling in less retardness is and will lead to less misery which is not happiness but still is less misery, though being renovated retard may give you lot more progressive things as you will facilities unfair exchange (i.e. exchange of things which doesn't have equivalent potential of progress and lead to retardness). If you understand above thing, you will understand why it is very easy make retard more retard and it is though to make retard realize that they have shown retardness and toughest to change retard (if they can and are trying to change) into default.

Remember one more quality of renovated retard other than what I discussed before is that they use other people thing without thinking twice, specially usage of piracy even piracy of nonsense (of there own or others) or to create nonsense for example they will talk about science or philosophy (if prior science) though there contribution is nothing and they lead to no progress still but to support there own nonsense they mould things (make them relative which doesn't mean anything though but retards think it does because of there delusion) or they simply pirate while moulding other or there own nonsense and you should do the same and you even mould my this books content for your own nonsense I have no problem until and unless I don't get to know about that, I would say make things more and more relative and make retard more and more retard, and you should collaborate with other renovated retards which will for sure increase you following doesn't matter whether you or people support or oppose that renovated retard because after all those thing retards will be forgot as that was baseless anyway and for baseless thing and will just keep following and it doesn't matter what do ever you talk on (nobody has every done anything progressive on the basis of relative talk-talk bullshit) and top of all remember it is the best time for renovated retard after 30 years for sure this time will be no more for renovated retards as when there will be number retard will be decreased a lot and no option for retardness to survive after that there will be no retards which in turn make sure that there will be no renovated retard left and new will not be formed overall which could take decades.

Chapter 7

Necessities of Every Brain

These are the necessities which brain want to be fulfilled and remember fulfilment of necessities is necessity in itself. The necessities here we going to talk about is universal without any exception for fit human being and these necessities are useful while creating any new thoughts or things whether it is food, cloths, buildings, businesses or any kind of invention and are also the parameters of carrying capacity.

1. Symmetry

Now I want you to understand what I mean by symmetry when I say symmetry it doesn't mean exactly that one line drawn so that it dived the whole thing into mirror image but through symmetry, I mean symmetry in whole but also symmetry in part of something, though still for this topic overall symmetry is our main concern for any particular thing. Symmetry can be seen in every human work because we like it as it is our necessity, but one may ask why? The reason is very simple as overall symmetric thing are easy and better to comprehend but why they are easy and better to comprehend? If you understand how we see and comprehend things then you will understand that

1. First, thinking is flow of thoughts it is best in flow to be more focused and concentrated and have better flow only when there is symmetry, but especially in seeing when our eye moves even when it seems like it is not moving even when you are looking towards a single word your eyes are constantly moving so you can understand brain creating image again and again because of this also and seeing in it self an ongoing process so if something is symmetric it is easy to create image as I told you thoughts are like flow but if some thing is not symmetric then

it become difficult to create image and create chaos as flow is not smooth off course it doesn't happened so you will not able to see but if something is really asymmetric for sure you will take more time to comprehend (comparatively) that thing off course you will be able to comprehend but you will start using your memory a lot to comprehend that's why if you really comprehend a asymmetric thing it is hard to forget it (look basically same size of asymmetric thing takes more bits of a particular unit symmetrical than symmetrical thing would).

2. Second reason is related to that of sight only, creating image is ongoing process because first eyes moves constantly and second is colours are seen through constant stimulation and that's why when we see thing we call something to be more asymmetric which has same colour rather than asymmetric thing which has different colour and that's why generally symmetry in a single colour every body like more than symmetry in different colour so basically when we see symmetry it don't create a chaos in our brain which means direction of flow changing again and again but if suddenly see asymmetric thing it does create a chaos in brain. Most of the thing is of same colour which are mostly overall symmetric.

3. Third reason is we are highly biased about seeing symmetry because all animal posse bilateral symmetry except porifera (which doesn't poses any symmetry overall) and mostly all Man made things posses overall symmetry (as symmetry is a better thing to formed in terms of copying, creating, comprehending and lasting for long) so as I told you thoughts are driven by circumstance we just like symmetry and we don't like overall asymmetric things in general until and unless a person other necessities take over this particular necessity for an instance.

4. In general overall asymmetric comprehension is more in itself for almost the same size of something else, it is simply the result of very existence of things, hence symmetry is preferred.

We don't call asymmetric thing asymmetric generally we call them ugly, unattractive, dangerous, unpleasant, nasty etc. For example, if we call a face beautiful then for sure that face must be very symmetric, we can easily understand or point out things as ugly even something go little bit out of symmetry so asymmetric face must be an ugly face and same goes with scary faces, they will for sure will not be symmetric. When it comes to other things you may think how come you like asymmetry in painting or something else? answer is nobody can like something which is completely asymmetric (it doesn't exist but here I mean very less symmetric) if I talk about painting (I am not talking about nonsense modern arts or something) then every painting has a balance of symmetry and asymmetry and at least it has one symmetry for sure that going to be it's boundary even if painting is asymmetric in itself it will never have asymmetric boundaries (if that the case for a painting that painting is nothing more the scam in name of art and progress specially if expensive which mostly the case) if it does have asymmetric boundaries and in itself in between has asymmetry nobody will like it. More or less of something to be preferred directly depend upon the symmetry also (other than other things) for example less the angle (considering one quadrant) or proximity of an asymmetric thing to line of symmetry more problematic it is. If person claim to like crazy asymmetric stuff, they will just pretend to like it because of different reasons as perfect asymmetric is just not fulfil of our necessity of symmetry in any way. So overall people like symmetry so more structural something (while following symmetry) better it is. As I told you I will tell you why people don't like jumbo bodybuilder the reason when a person start training his/her body (as they say) they can't go with perfect training so that they can't train every muscle equally (nor production, consumption and efficiency of anything is same every where) because of which there body start looking asymmetric as there bilateral symmetry become distorted (at least) and that's why people don't like big jumbo (though lot of disproportion will also talk place).

Author's Note – There is no such thing like asymmetric thing which is mostly considered opposite of symmetry, there is nothing in this world which doesn't follow even a bit of line of symmetry but of course some bodies have a line of symmetry for the whole body but some doesn't have that one single line of symmetry for the whole body but of course if you zoom in you will find line of symmetry for something even then also you doesn't (though you can keep doing that) then at least the way you zoom in form line of symmetry for example you can zoom in this book (if eBook) on any blank spot then line of symmetry will be formed on it's own as the boundary of your zoom in itself will be following symmetry in it self and if not than again you can do the same thing and you find one or when you will reach at any particle level you will find symmetry but it will always be impossible for purely asymmetric thing (or asymmetry not only in terms of word but in reality) to exist nor I know how it would be like but for sure reality has no opposite other wise it would no be absolute but will become relative at least and that would be contradictory and reality has no contradiction. So here we are just talking about more or less line of symmetry and specially a single line of symmetry present or not to use the term asymmetric or symmetric. Though in comparison you can use the word asymmetric for two different symmetries just to refer to that very comparison which is real (absolute) origin of word asymmetric (Disproportion is nothing more than different symmetry comparison).

PS – There is no doubt in that beauty is something everybody likes and there is no doubt in that either that people are highly confused about what is more beautiful or try to make some nonsense, specially they confuse things to be more beautiful with being more accessible or stimulating for them self in particular way. I want to be clear about this, for similar things which are more beautiful are more accessible and overall, more stimulating but they can be less for you in the sense that you don't interact with them that much or can't because of whatsoever reason and something which is more accessible or stimulating (in any way or overall) is not necessarily more beautiful (though remember better stimulation is not about just more it is also about the consistency and convergence while obviously within limits). So, for example cube and a ring of same material is equally beautiful but one of them can be more accessible (like a cloth of perfect fitting for you) or stimulating according to certain scenario, similarly whiter colour (let say in skin) is not more beautiful but defiantly is more stimulating and can make person more accessible (let say to point out in crowd of less white or to more colours of clothing to again look more stimulating or being more accessible).

I want to be very clear about this that is to say something is better looking then you have to exactly define the parameters and accountability of them and there is no doubt in that parameter will overlap (and obviously don't try to create nonsense like I am significantly fat but I am not ugly or I don't have any accessibility problem or I am just fine/better etc.). When it is question of beauty then it is just about symmetry but again parameters overlap, especially it is very important to understand mostly beauty and stimulation has not so much to do with what person as if you are fit, for example you can see properly then what is more beautiful it is more beautiful and stimulating visually for me and you (it is not about certain different relation), the only things which can different significantly even when you are fit is accessibility not only accessibility of a certain thing in itself but also what you are in the sense what exact you cope up with (though it is important to under if you are fit them very design aspect of that thing for accessibility will not be too much different to be more accessible to me or by you). Though when I say accessibility can be bit different significantly that no way means it can contradict other parameters and it is independents of those parameters instead it would be directly be dependent on those very significantly for example less stimulation (or less symmetry) of something in itself or similar stimulation (or similar symmetry proportions) of something in itself which act as a boundary between different characteristics will significantly decrease the accessibility aspect (individually and simultaneously) of those characteristics (and definitely there is no such thing like accountability of nonsense).

2. New

Every person want new things again and again but why we want new thing does it is really necessary to have new thing? and till now if you don't asked yourself why progress is important then you can self evaluate yourself, what you are? Progress is important not because we are on some mission (hollow term) or it is just a rule who do progress is a thinker or normal and one should be like them. Answer is very simply progress mean creating new (not necessarily by being a thinker coping a new is still creating new for yourself) and to have access to new is necessity of us specially because of a simple biggest reason we have memory and there is no doubt we have quite strong memory, now because of memory when we see a thing again and again we become biased about that thing and we start assuming it to be like that only what we have seen before for example if you read this book 4-5 times you will start skipping words because your brain will assume it is the same as before whether you remember the whole book word by word or not or if book is changed a bit and reading this book will stimulate your brain less effectivity than what it use to do before (also because you already know that stuff after a read) and we need constant stimulation from time to time but why we need constant stimulation? Biggest direct reason is because we have memory if somebody is born blind than that person will not crave for seeing colours or beautiful view or something as his/her brain structure will not developed in that way so even if a person is not born blind but kept in dark for 7-8 years will also not crave for light and being exposed to light he/she will not able to see light properly to comprehend together, also would take some time to develop brain in a way so he/she can properly see and react and crave for that kind of stimulation (so obviously if you have brain with a particular brain structure you need stimulation accordingly as till you are alive brain going to be an constant stimulation).

But old thing can become new (to some extent) if after some time you lose memories about that particular thing or its particular things and then that thing will again stimulate you properly (more). In general, if something is not used by you which you don't used quite often will become new again after 3 months to 1 years (you had stopped using it). Every necessity we are going to about or talked about when fulfilled make people happy after all you feel happy or sad when you think it is necessary to fell so, but the most important one is fulfilling necessity of new and that obvious also because thing should be there at the first place to fulfil any kind of necessity, people feel really crazy happy when they create or modify something which nobody has done before (even if that's not the case) that's why retard and renovated retard are never remain happy in there life because they don't do anything new really on there own nor cope up with the progress. And there is no doubt in that if you don't want anything new and if you are satisfied that simply means you are dead or a retard (who suffers from delusions).

One of the most important things to keep in mind is that if you got memory of something then you will use it at least a bit while thinking of related things as whole brain is connected. Another most important thing to consider is comparison and usage or inclination towards memory. So for example if a person who is already miserable (because of less stimulation to fulfil necessity), then when that person experience something which in itself is lot more stimulating which make him/her very happy then that person will become more miserable for sure if that person return to prior scenario because of many reason like that person will ignore that (prior) level stimulation more because he/she got memory of something which is way more, not only that prior stimulation in itself it is very less to make a person happy so inclination towards memory will become even more and that person would have a felling of lacking, top of all memory is not same stimulating as that of direct stimulation which was experienced and also because memory has to be refreshed to be maintained, hence that person memory will simply fade more quickly and that person would be overall more miserable. But if a person who is already experiencing happiness (because of more stimulation) then when that person experience something which in itself is lot more stimulating which make him/her very happy then that person most probably going to be more happy or at least not miserable by any means when he/she will return to prior scenario, as that person inclination to memory to cut or ignore direct stimulation is very less because that person scenario already have enough stimulation making him happy as it in itself it is not less compared to basic fulfilment needed as a person, so overall most probably that person will use that memory to combined with direct stimulations and will become more happy, not only that that memory will not fade like crazy instead of that person will have more happy memory to make him/her more happy because of connecting all, that's why most probably it will not create the felling of lacking if that person is progressive. In the example of first person, you can consider things like pseudo experience, addiction and overall progression of becoming more retard (and miserable). Remember comparison is not some relative bullshit.

Another reason why new is important is because it is needed obviously because to survive as not only for overall progress but also to not get retarded or to maintain a certain system, so not necessarily for just being progressive for example maintaining yourself you need more and more things which is new in itself in comparison to what you had before specially because of different quantity and obviously because of efficiency at any given period (though here in particularly for the necessity we are talking new category wise). But obviously overall progress is necessary for survival and for happiness but certainly that has lot to do with periods, comparison and competition.

Creating new thing are very easy if you understand the necessity for progress overall and that's what we are talking about in this book. But one must remember to create new thing you must explore every new thing that's how you going to know what can be the next and what you have created is exactly new or not for world and if it new then how. There is no doubt in that new progressive things always work to create the necessity of new for example phone - nobody need to advertisement that every body should have a phone off course marketing a brand is a different thing but then again a brand which always come up with new modification don't need advertisement of their brand name everybody will know them and what they do and that's why it has become so called brand at the first place (though internet for most part is very retarding). Write now retail market to show crazy retardness work on very simple concept of relativity they show useful, worthless, more worthless, more and more worthless product and retards are becoming more and more retard and crossing all limit of retardness so depending upon what they see they chose in-between worthless product to fulfil there desire of rolling in retardness and fulfilling necessity of new (not really but it's a futile attempt) so again very easy to rise as renovated retard and need less to say what retard buy online many time even they don't use it and even don't open it at the first place more than what they do in offline, obviously in online in which they have to think less that is more better and can produce more delusion of new, specially through pseudo experience.

3. Space

First, what is space and how much big space? Answer is space (by big I mean more in terms of what more or less can almost be explore together by human being) is an absolute terms, so big enough to fulfil necessities but than why necessities are about space? Answer is very simple space is something which our brain and body wants but why and how much in particular? To understand that why our brain want space as why our body need space is quite obvious, we have to understand two things, first - how we concentrate and second - how we relax, to understand how we concentrate first we have to understand on what we concentrate and why? We concentrate on thing so we can comprehend them, do different things and for creating new things (more space) which means we restrict the flow of thinking in particular directions but then you can't stop the flow of thought and overall therefore you can't focus on thing more than a particular time period and we do this by using our senses and brain, most important of all senses is seeing for concentrating (which is obvious), if you concentrate then suddenly you contract your eye and make you focus on that point only and try to cut other vison and all of your senses more or less diverge there sensibility towards the thing more which means ignoring other stimulation as you are trying to restrict the flow of thoughts in particular directions because your brain start giving more importance to that particular thing you are focusing on, but this do help us to concentrate but this also cause fatigue and from here the necessity of enough space came into role-play more than ever because to relax you have to do just completely different of what you were doing which is - not restricting the flow, making the flow smooth which means relaxing your eyes, make all your senses back to comprehend more than comprehend less (but more superficially, which is very important to explore more because if you doesn't really have thing to explore at the first place how will get to particular thing to concentrate on, hence very important for more creativity), rather then wanting to explore something particular and better but this can only happen if you are now focused toward something big in size (or superficially more). If your in small area then you will not be able to relax well and because of which when you will try to concentrate on something even when you doesn't want to as you doesn't have an other option, your concentration will decrease with every cycle and after some time you will not able to concentrate even a bit and obviously will become less and less creative even if you were creative before.

If you have doubt in that then you can try on your own sit in a corner while facing toward the Corner concentrate on something particular then when you feel fatigue then look only at corner nothing else and don't change position after some cycles you will not able to concentrate again. Now question arises exactly how big (here we are just concerned about living space)? answer is at least more than 20 feet is more than enough in open free space to as far you want to fulfil necessity for relaxing in every sense (and concentrating in between and with them), so physically at least a person in every three days should in that for an hour for feeling pleasant, you may ask why a three-day cycle? it is according to memory so specially once in week in free space become very necessary. Remember mammals took over the earth very quickly because of two biggest reason first proper thermal regulation and second, they move like crazy and obviously more moving gives you more big things and new things. If you have a question about how much space is need to create a better home in which for sure you are going to happy and creative enough to cope up with progress then answer is 1000sq.ft per person, this is applicable till 6 person.

As I told you I will talk about absolutist, one of the thing which absolutist will never do is making an argument against argument or answer an argument with just information specially which is not confined by knowledge (and obviously not using nonsense) because argument can never be an knowledge nor they are necessarily is information confined by knowledge even if they are not relative bullshit or relative or bullshit (mostly a person who calls himself or herself a sceptic do things like that and mostly people who call themselves sceptic are the worst idiotic so obviously become significant renovated retard), problem with that is even if an argument against argument is real information confined by knowledge then also it doesn't exactly help you with knowledge nor its progressive, it is not possible to answer an argument which is nonsense nor it is possible to make argument against it without making an relative or relative bullshit or directly considering bullshit and calling it an argument against the argument. One of thing which people doesn't understand specially the people who call them self sceptic is there is no such thing like unreal so there is no possible way of contradicting it for real and relative or relative bullshit or direct bullshit are only contradicted by real information (i.e. something which refer to something or is something it self) only in the sense that's it's directly point out the information of some scenario or the whole scenario but that is not something which has anything to do with relative or relative bullshit or bullshit (all that is generally called answering to argument or dissolving an argument not an argument against argument), hence even if argument is an relative or relative bullshit or bullshit or not it can't lead to progress and specially while making argument against relative or relative bullshit or bullshit you yourself will create another relative or relative bullshit or bullshit though that would not be done by absolutist but would create more nonsense and will make nonsense famous. Absolutist will only point out for an argument to be relative or relative bullshit or bullshit without using real information or knowledge and specially will only focus to lay knowledge directly as information can always be fetched from it.

There are some renovated retard who say money doesn't matter or be happy with small or something like that but let me tell you money is not currency it is the things which surround you and around you and you yourself is money (quiet frankly everything is money and best money definition can't be more than - what can be exchange thus every information is money as it is about interaction and there is no contradiction to information and interaction) and if it is the question of currency than it is nothing in itself (obviously just an interface, though to have any information - there have to be money or basically it's all about stuff) today it is just a way to access thing (money) or own them, (overall everything is about interaction - again no contradiction to that), again in this whole topic of space I am not trying to convey that you should own more and more spacious thing (basically making an relative bullshit) but I am try to convey that you should be that much able so you can access (interact) the spacious things enough to fulfil necessity at least. The funniest thing is the people who say money don't matter or is an unnecessary how retard they are that they don't understand to say that also it should be necessary that there are thinking about money only as no unnecessary thought popup in anybody brain and again as any progressive person will or use to say (or at least that what is necessity) that they want access to the great things and thoughts.

Every thing is money i.e. space, if there is question of having currency power then if somebody create new or modified thing or cope up with the progress (money) how come that person wouldn't have currency power? Currency is nothing more than exchanging power, obviously retards doesn't have that as they created nothing and doesn't cope up with progress so how come they think they should have a crazy exchanging power and if retards have any currency, then mostly it is about getting the benefits of the progress which they never did or cope up with. If anybody think this book is about materialism than you are not in a delusion i.e., thinking that you can think without material or you can think of any other thing than material. If somebody doubt the concept of space then they can check on there own most happy counties and place where people are happy (i.e. significant percentage of people are happy) have less population density (and basically have more stuff and stuff is spacious enough) and any renovated retard ever rise - they rise from high population density because people living in high population density are miserable and any gang every formed is also formed in high populated areas only and renovated retards rise from there and where population density high and less stuff is there - there religion dominate because if person is miserable that person is a retard and retard are religious (we have already talked about that) off course religion don't make people retard, retard people make religion and retard people follow religion. The most important is that so called people who will say they do good, right for people will only be found in high population density only and so-called people who do bad, wrong for people are also found there only the most as it just relative bullshit of retards (Progress people are not interested in talking about doing this or that for people in anyway).

And for today's world quiet important thing for example phone or for any thing else one must at least understand the necessity of space for creativity and for relaxing the brain and for proper cycle of concentration, for example when you use phone it reduce concentration and make brain go crazy, make brain fatigue as when you use phone to watch something, from some sense it give brain the message you are in something more spacious and part of it, from another it give the message you are concentrating as it is less spacious and you are part of something small so basically brain try to relax and concentrate at the same time (which means doing back forth of relaxing and concentrating) which delay initial fatigue but after some time cause a more bigger and intense fatigue to brain and can easily make you feel frustrated which will overall lead to low concertation and less creativity in long term.

4. Smooth and Shiny

Though you must be knowing this before hand everyone is attracted toward smooth and shiny thing because most show their attraction towards smooth and shinny things more freely in between at least some people than anything but then also they are some retards who even have a problem in this also who call these kind of thing evil or illusion or delusion, though we already discussed why there is nothing like evil as it is relative bullshit, we will discuss more about it and there is no doubt in that these thing are real (and there is no nonsense in that they are more stimulating). Retard start saying this because they them self also like these kind of thing but they never able to have them or access them sufficiently (specially considering the continuous progress) because they are worthless but then there kids and other relative start demanding for that and there own necessities of having these thing lead them to jealousy and envy so to hide their incapability and there feeling of lacking it lead to saying these thing are evil (reasoning - why it is evil? Because it should not be present why it should be present? Because it evil or simply say it is unreal hence delusion or illusion which you shouldn't think of as it is unreal), in between renovated retard came in as they always rise from misery and start opposing these kinds of things (smooth and shiny) and start saying one should not to be attracted towards these kind of thing (specially as they may say this 'outer' beauty which is just relative or relative bullshit or bullshit anyway) and again as always renovated retard gained popularity as I told you it is very easy to become a renovated retard.

Once I heard a renovated retard Indian guru who have millions of follower (when I was 7.4) saying that the pretty girls who have smooth, shiny skin (who are also very beautiful) are delusion so nobody should be attracted to them and no-one should interact with them even not verbally, god (relative bullshit at best) made them for distraction, so that's very obvious his follower who are nodding head and he himself doesn't understand delusion meaning (they make it relative bullshit) and are jealous (obviously most retards are unfit and unfit looks ugly for sure and they are trying to be against the reality and obviously progress), as I told you all beautiful things is about symmetry, some people are against it too. We are going to talk about smooth things though generally all smooth thing is shiny (visually) which obviously you will be if you are fit and thing would be if they are more stimulating. If the question about other unfit people arises, is it their fault, they are ugly? It doesn't matter who's fault it is (ugly is just ugly), so let me tell you there is no doubt in that less than 5% kids are born with some disabilities mentally and physically but then most of people who are not born with disability they become very retarding physically and mentally on there own, though I would preferably say this more believingly before 1950 and more easily because today I believe many more people (percentage wise and obviously for sure number wise) are just born unfit or very less fit (still most are born fit) which is often not considerable but most important thing is prior or present retards (specially unfit) who were or are not whipped out properly give rise to more retards (specially unfit both mentally and physically) in population.

Now lets talk about why smooth and shiny are necessity and obviously better, to understand that first you must understand the most important sense is sense of sight and then second most important sense is touch. If we talk about why so -we like that kind of thing? I think it very easy to understand it stimulate our brain in a uniform manner which don't create a chaos or random (not so systematic) stimulation which obviously is better because this kind of stimulation make sure our focus doesn't go here and there randomly just like a turbulent flow which make us feel retarding so basically smooth and shiny thing stimulate our brain in systematic manner (and obviously are more symmetric so all point of symmetric are valid here too). Ad I told you earlier that thoughts are like flow so you can understand what smooth and shiny does is that keep that flow of thoughts very systematic without any chaos (and that's why smooth and shiny thing in one colour or in one material is more better because you can understand flow will be better), unlike rough things which cause crazy flow here and there of thoughts and that's trouble for brain even though for sometime flow can go cray like that but after that brain will become tired fast but in smooth and shiny thing flow is maintain properly and because of which it doesn't make brain tired fast but instead of that it make us feel pleasant (limits implied), so you can understand it is mainly about the flow so even something is not so smooth then also if it follow some kind of systematic flow which causes systematic flow in our brain then also we can like that thing. But that not the only thing smooth and shiny thing gives more stimulation as per sight sense because of more light and as per the touch sense because it has more perfect touch sensation because of being even and more contact area.

So human brain by default prefer more systematic and symmetric pattern over something which has no such bigger pattern (not in the sense of contradicting interaction but as overall system and symmetry), but there people who try to contradict thing like that and overall that's why most of the people are not capable creating new thing which as just try to think in terms of already know (prior) menial pattern at best (if they are not delusional) and that's why having higher IQ has no as such advantage because it is just by default mode not doing more work to go against the default mode of menial patter following specially which are not really new (too much of remembering patterns basically just information is not useful but instead they are in the way of more creativity).

All people like smooth and shiny thing you can't break this because it is created because of ongoing process of using senses nor you have to break it (like you poke your eyes) because it gives you pleasant feeling so it's just better but you can easily break other biases of pattern and that what absolutism is and that what has potential to make you a thinker for example if somebody say hello to you then you will reply what you think absolutely rather then just saying hello because it is what norms says or rule is (instead you will confine information by knowledge then take it any way to take any action, if not possible then simply discard it), if everybody is standing you should think why to stand at the first place is it a information confined by knowledge or it is just an rule or law so until you think you doesn't got reason of it being information confined by knowledge to stand don't stand if you were sitting, if every body think something is difficult or easy then you must consider it as nothing until and under you really considering that thing and coming to an result. Though those things make you absolutist for certain things but that doesn't mean you are always being an absolutist and no way means you are coping up with the progress but then you will break your own pattern of doing things and rolling in nonsense (and doing retardness) while you find knowledge and information confined by knowledge by your own way or you will create your own thing or cope up with the progress which will make you a thinker or normal or default absolutist. So, in short don't go with the flow suddenly at the instance.

As I told you people don't like jumbo bodybuilder another reason is that because when a person has very profound looking muscle it make there body look like it is not smooth because of which people will not like them as it will be having more angles. And if we talk about face and body as I told you beautiful face and body are the symmetric one but if face have more angles, corners, disproportion in body and face (especially bigger body to face ratio), rough then it starts looking less attractive i.e., less stimulating or accessible (or not cute as some people would say).

Authors Note- There is no such thing like rough which is opposite of smooth as here we are using here term smooth only according to our receptors getting even stimulation simultaneously without break so there is no break in flow of thoughts or turbulent flow of thoughts for more stimulation so we can use this instead of using the term smooth and shiny as we are talking about reality so it is absolute we can define it absolutely and it is not relative and for sure a so called rough according to our receptor while zooming in and for different small area for different receptors will be smooth but there can't be a purely rough surface even I myself doesn't know what that can be because it is not presently in reality. Again reality doesn't have any relative or relative bullshit thing that exist so opposite of reality can't exist other wise it would be contradictory. Ask your self can you really think opposite of your face or something else.

5. Sex and Food

Every body like food and sex whether a person except it or not but why we like this? because our brain is formed in that way that we always searching for a mate and food because that's what the reason is we are present today otherwise through natural selection we will not going to be present today and that's something obvious survival of species depend on it descends and food. But then more renovated retard and retard are there-they talk more nonsense, let's consider some of there nonsense, first about food - you will find many retards and renovated retard saying be prudent because it is good, ethical, all other animal are prudent or some another direct bullshit reason. First let me tell you there is nothing like being prudent nor any animal is prudent mean anything, some people refer to being prudent as a lion will kill only one deer out of group of deer because it is prudent therefore lion kills prey according to how much it need (what a joke), a lion never eat the whole of the animal nor all other animal eat the whole of animal killed by them nor necessarily kill one nor that has anything to do with thinking of being prudent or something and that's why scavenger exist (and whatsoever they ate they doesn't use it all even if they more than usual so finishing something is just retardness if is for nonsense or just result of other retardness, obviously to be crazy fat you have to ate more - considering the limit according to body efficiency and being crazy fat is just the result of retards getting benefits of progress) and if a person called being prudent is killing just one animal or getting more then not eating all of it (non- veg or veg) (it's not a thinking of any kind) then all human being are prudent too (even retards to a certain extant) because nobody order 10-20 people food for himself/herself alone (though still it's bit relative), after that leaving some of the food is not wastage nor it make us some kind of evil (reasoning - it should not be there because it is evil and it is evil because it should not be there) and again anybody think that left over food is wasted then let me tell it all used for this or that purpose (nothing is retarding until and unless it retard the progress like being overpopulated and majority being retard is the most retarding) and earth is not shrinking because somebody is or is not prudent or because he/she is that or this kind of prudent (and those things doesn't make sense in any way for carrying capacity) and do let me know if that is happening.

You can easily find people who will tell you not to be foody not to eat different type of food, stick to one. Let me tell you if you don't eat different type of food stick to one for sure it will affect you not only physically but also mentally and it already shown by different studies how different thing are important for healthy brain and that obvious too. Off course I am not talking about being a crazy fat person if you are crazy fat, you are a retard. Another joke I know which is created some few years ago only started with some countries i.e. there are ugly(asymmetric) vegetable which people don't use or grocery store don't buy so that they go into waste or some kind of waste is happening or some partiality is going on, again what a joke, now you can understand as I told you it very easy to become an renovated retard this is an great example of that, let me tell you people don't throw vegetable just because they are ugly these are used by restaurant for making food, sauces etc. Or used in any other kind of purposes or sold in local market and again do let me know if earth is shrinking or we are retarding the progress because we wasted ugly vegetables. Let me tell you one more relative bullshit i.e. junk food which are very harmful or less nutritious taste the best (answer is obviously no), basically what have better nutrients have better taste and more different thing you can use together to make better taste (basically blend together) - better it is, most people mostly eat food which is less tasty and hence they try to cop up with this fact by adding more sugar, salt, spices etc. not only that they try to cop up with there overall miserable life with that (we will talk about addiction later). I don't wonder why this is an famous relative bullshit because just take any thing which most people right now is clamming to like to have regularly it is basically menial or basically in simple word for two most cultural thing i.e. food and cloth it would be more of one piece of one thing concept as religion is against any progress and most people can't be religious about any other than some menial thing, after all retards are 'retard' they can't think, have or do better on there own.

Now let's talk about sex, you will find many renovated retard who will tell you not to do sex or just do it to produce kids or something like that, first let me tell you sex is not harmful instead of that is useful for being healthy mentally and physically, and top all according to some surveys the highly successful people (not just sexually) have high sex drive and studies suggest they live even 1-8 year more, my point is very simple if you are living and you hate sex or don't have a drive for sex for sure you are retard worthless for progress and you are unfit to survive (for sure at least sexually). Though the most funny thing the gurus (renovated retards) and other retard who opposed sex I think they have forget that even though nobody asked there witch mother how many times they have been fucked result of which there are produced but that doesn't mean it was an one time thing or they are produced by some sort of so called witch magic or any progress is done because of there nonsense talking. Off course I am not supporting any kind of multi partner practice through this. One must remember sex and food are the biggest direct pleasure and that obvious too as both are equally important for continuation of any species.

One of the retards genius thing (basically relative bullshit) is to say they opt not to chose particular things (even which are very necessary for progress or very basic for well being) because of some relative bullshit (or any nonsense) reasoning, especially it is not like they does opt to chose to not to chose but they don't have an option at the first place and then to try to make there point they did have the option before hand and specially whenever they will have an option they will not chose it to show crazy retardness or make sure they will never have an option. Retards go to great extent to prove the above point which obviously cause more misery best example of that will be creating relative bullshit on the food or sex alike to say - don't have sex other than to have kids or just never do it, don't do sex in position which gives more pleasure or just try not to have pleasure, cut your penis fore skin or vaginal lips or clitoris, don't eat different food - stick to menial food, starve or do so called dieting, destroying tongue either by cutting or burning, etc.

6. Partial Dependency

This one is the most effective one because it can take all five prior necessities and other necessities under it, it is the supreme of stimulation, if some thing is partial dependent on you then you are on it too, you will enjoy it the most, first- one must understand one can show partial dependency not equally to all thing in some cases it will be better and in some not so strong as different thing fulfil different necessities and different thing are different but generally partial dependency is the most in which above five necessities are fulfilled (all of them) and other necessities in particular are fulfilled so overall there going to be only one thing which really would have partial decency the best with you, but why we want to be partial dependent and exactly what it is? First I want you to understand this necessity doesn't exist on it's own so it really not important one to be partially dependent on some thing but you will be time to time because it is about stuffs and specially you will be as fit member of species for continuation of species (because to live/survive you have to explore stuffs other than your self) and as I told you it give lot of stimulation so we tend to become partially dependent and if we talk about what exactly it is - then it is an cycle of stimulation, though it should be obvious it is different from being dependent and independent but then also most important thing what make partial dependency different is that is continuous but yet not continuous on it own as it is the result of series of events and have series of event (interactions) which is in between and about a person and a thing or another person and not necessarily to be for and about same thing every time.

Off course, you can call partial dependency as love (if you define it as synonym) but some people call only one part of it as love when it is between human and human that simply means making it relative so love don't exist if it is relative and if love exist than it is the whole partial dependency (absolutely). Let's take some example first let talk about within human to human, these are only made when both of the human are partial dependent on each other - that's when ever so called love it is there should be partial dependency, for example – lot of parent love there kids because they have partial dependent bond in between, parent love them when there kids fulfil the partial dependency and when they fulfil it properly which means special consideration from 4-12 as before 4 they show very little of partial dependency by less giving responses to action through action (interaction) and are dependent for lot of things as they don't do there work on there own even little properly or not able to do, but after 12 kids become more independent more than partially dependent (and specially better partial dependency in adults is better formed in same age group specially with complimentary gender) so again loves goes down after 18-25 of age in between parents and children which are not kids any more, become independent so love (partial dependency) goes almost zero, now it depend whether they live together or not and etc. Though in today's world descents don't become overall independent after 25 also because they have crossed all the limit of retardness you check on your own almost 50% millennials earn less than there parent and even live in there parent home and even there parent pay there student loan (also give them so-called allowance) sometimes even after they got the degree and if you wonder when this kind of retardness more than ever started that peoples kids start earning or doing less than there parent (in the most significantly manner) then the answer is after 1950 and specially as I said as people go retard more retarding they do and again one can't ignore the fact that most of the money directly or indirectly is handled by millennials only which means most of people are going worthless which mean they are retard (don't forget we are way overpopulated) and some of them are thinker and normal and renovated retard as this is the best period for these categories to rise.

Many people may think we have some kind of ethics (what relative bullshit that is I don't know as there are lot of version of that but something which people use to support some particular bullshit or relative bullshit) or some other things which lead us to love (there love definition which is nonsense) or living together then let me tell you there is nothing like ethics or something else because of which we live together, we live together with family or whatever as it is purely a selfish reason of having partial dependency (in simple words fulfilling necessities which you can call mean or selfish but that what we are, we are mean or selfish as even if you say that you or anybody else is/are not mean/selfish than also you are mean and everybody else too because that what you say and if somebody say you are not mean than also you are mean because that's what only way somebody would say something about you, until you exist and you exist so till then you are mean or selfish and after that there is no you, obviously people can make relative bullshit of terms like selfish for example if you don't give me something particular even though it will be unfair exchange or you say the reality which obviously a retard would not like then you are mean or selfish).

Basically majority i.e., retards want to get the benefit of the progress they never did nor cop up with by making relative bullshit like kindness, good, ethical etc. Let me tell you before Neanderthals (Homo sapiens neanderthalensis) most probably no hominins use to live together from the start to the end and that obvious because most probably before Neanderthal no species like us is able to communicate properly as Neanderthal are first one capable of speaking really (with great precession and accuracy) as they have lot of similar kind of structure what we have and the concept of god and ghost are also something which is also started by them only because they have speaking skill which is the best communication skill, so basically retard Neanderthal created that concept and lot of our species (Homo sapiens sapiens) interacted with them with there own nonsense and shared nonsense stories, retarding concept which off course means culture (religious bullshit) and obviously progressive things too.

There is no doubt concept of rules, regulation, god, ghost and laws were created when human start lacking reasoning that's why they are considered to be the biggest reason to support or oppose anything by retards humans. And you can see on your own any species which live together they live for benefits (fulfilling necessities) and they have some kind of communication skill without it no population (which always about species) will live together. You will find many retard who will say love is beautiful, good, ethical, only a human thing, can't be with any non living thing, let me tell you that love is not beautiful because there is nothing like love there is just partial dependency which you can call love but off course the person you love can be beautiful, very stimulating and accessible (symmetric face, body and smooth and shinny skin and some other things) but retard get retard only and that's why there partial dependency is messed up always (more or less they just lose it very fast, if they ever got into one), again there is nothing right, wrong, good, bad, ethical, unethical in partial dependency (obviously mostly it is for direct progress), and if we talk about being in love with non-living than the best example of that is thinkers as they generally they don't want be even in partially dependent with menial things (sometime not even with humans, though partial dependency with human can easily be the most stimulating one) and most things because it is hard to find complementary to be more progressive (that doesn't means any interaction is necessarily retarding) and they show partial dependency on things, their partial dependency is one of the best one as it is formed while they are trying to create something new in that process they give lot of attempt to reach the result in the attempt in which they didn't got the result they wanted but still they get stimulation as something has happened not what he/she seeking for but something different which creates a cycle of stimulation and again this is one of the best partial dependency because it's end is always happy even though it fetch result or not immediately.

There is no doubt the best (most fulfilling one) partial dependency a human can ever experience is with human partner only (of complementary gender) as they fulfil all five necessities which we have talked before and many other specially because being is almost same in age and other condition (like species and may be overall scenario). There is no doubt in that retard marriages can never go well as they lack everything included thoughts and work for coping up with progress, renovated retard marriage can go less messy as they have more open filed as they have significantly more things then retard, and thinkers marriages may or may not go well but normal and specially default people marriages mostly go well, if a person is normal for sure he/she can enjoy there marriage the most. One question everybody (particularly retards) asks or think on i.e., that person love me or does he/she still love me? I think you must have got the answer partial dependency is love (if want to really define love) so if it is not there in between there is nothing like love and there is nothing like one way or two-way partial dependency either it is there or it is not. And there is no such thing like unconditional love (partial dependency) because unconditional means unnecessary and unnecessary nobody can think nor can do. Quiet frankly relative bullshit thing like that on the name of love is direct relative bullshit of interaction and change (hence obviously contradictory to them).

7. General Biases Which Can't Be Broken

We are taking some things differently because there more or less is not a factor to be considered for our consideration. First bias I want to talk about is shape, we are biased about the particular shape but in that we are biased about something particular to understand that I want you to image a book bigger than the size of earth, have you imagined? If so then you must not have imagined a cube like book, you must have imagined a cuboid like book, but that bias is easy to break if I now say you to imagine cube like book you will able to do so and question of thinking bigger than earth than obviously more or less of thinking is about more or less of thinking not about other object (comparison in thinking is comparison of thinking only) but I am not talking about those bias or delusion instead I am talking about the bias of depth or what you may call breath (and other about shape discussed in 2nd book) and more or less about some sort of plural (or you can say overall biases we are going to about is about more connecting by default). Everyone is biased about imaging thing with some depth (information confined to make some sort of structure) as we haven't seen a perfectly flat surface as it don't exist, every thing has thickness - we know paper are thin but we still know they have some thickness and we can imagine a paper from side view and that's not only thing we understand depth by many ways (this biases is about connecting to have a structure), for example by looking directly towards the object or by looking at the shadow and light source we can still understand depth of object because we have seen so many light sources and shadows, another way is trough wind by using our skin as we stood near by so many thing in our life while wind blow we get an idea of depth through that (and off course we understand more and less stimulation and stimulation at particular point and through particular things), another way is through sound which you must be familiar with more profoundly because of your driving skill but sound not only tell you how far thing is but also tell you how thick and what kind of that thing is because we have experience how sound travel in different object of different thickness and how sound bounce back, another way is through speed of two object you find the gap between two thing by seeing how they were moving next to each other. But this bias and overall bias of ours make us feel uncomfortable with things which are not so less thick usually but if we see them as becoming less thick, we don't like it for example a so-called flat face, a flat cake, a flat person or any kind of a flat thing which are not usually flat. The most import use of this bias can be to make some thing new even two thing are same but one has more depth it will look new to us for example if there is land which continuous but in between you just make little part of it elevate a little bit you will feel it is something new or different and you will have different feeling at that point.

The second bias we can't break is bias of motion we highly biased about motion (basically more motion) because we understand motion through different senses (other than that reason is everything is in motion), for example understanding motion through seeing objects, light sources, shadow, through sound, smell and motion inside the body whether it is peristalsis or hiccups, heartbeat, breathing etc. That's why when we imagine any thing we imagine it with steps in which we make a imagination step by step and that's why we can't hold any kind of static image in our brain in comparison to other thinking kin sense of connecting) and if you can for long time for sure you are gone crazy/retard basically highly delusion (thinking in itself is motion). The most important thing is any thing which make us in more profound motion or in lot more motion itself - stimulate us a lot. The another bias we can't brake (which is part of motion bias) is bias of comparative stimulation on the sight or basically connecting thing, as I told you earlier we can't go for relative biases as they are not biased on bases of something or about something but comparative bias of stimulation on the sight or any way thing about two stuff nobody can break because it is the matter of thing being together and together means together and it is matter of very small period so every body got into this thinking for a instance.

Another bias we can't break (which the part of motion bias) is flow of thoughts even when there is no stimulation from out side brain we use memory and (again) quick connection of two things like direct on site comparison (for example of colours). One must remember brain only use memory a lot when it stop taking lot of direct stimulation from out side, you can't do both thing at the same time and that's why all hallucination (connecting memory with slight bit outside stimulation) happen to people in certain ways like ghost appearing from nowhere in dark because (dark means less or almost no outside stimulation) or private meeting to god or ghost or whatever, so brain use memory that's why hallucination generally happen in less stimulation, another thing which we can talk on this is black generally pure black don't exist (a object which has no reflection or 100% absorption) and black colour is no colour as it is about no stimulation as when you say you see pure black that would simply mean you are not seeing at all, that's why nobody can like or dislike or understand black colour in itself as it is just an hollow terminology (don't forget there is something known as reflection) and black magic is called black because of same reason and considered as bad, though magic and bad both don't exist and that's why generally black animals like cats etc. Are consider bad thought it is not bad but just no stimulation (if you say pure black) or less stimulation (if not pure black which basically means less white) off course we like stimulation and we consider more stimulation as better even though people can't like black in particular but you may heard people saying they like black colour it basically means they like any other colour as they like something else for example generally every body like black and white combination because of very simple reason white is very stimulating and black is not at all stimulating (if pure black, obviously don't forget about reflection), I just told you we have a habit of seeing thing and comparing them at an instance as seeing colour is an ongoing process so everybody would consider black and white as better then most of combination (especially useful defining boundaries for characteristics), another reason for which people say they like black colour would be he or she like white as I told you before hand pure black doesn't exist (nor there is a black colour) as some what you can say reflection is always there so instead of too much of stimulation of white directly from pure or way more white people may like have less white through reflection of so called black thing or colour. So basically, when you call things or people black coloured instead of that you should call them less white as black colour is a hollow terminology (nonsense – relative bullshit).

Author's note – After reading all this you must have understood without them (fulfilling necessity) or having lots of delusion (i.e., thinking to be able to think even though when you can't) will always create misery. I heard lots of renovated retards or retards saying kids are always happy they doesn't need any thing or a lot and bla bla bla. First - any of the above things (necessities) mentioned is important for any kid too, and to understand that well if want to ask you some questions like - do you ever saw a kid seeing an asymmetric face (or ugly face) for the first time and becoming happy? You will never as symmetry is important. Do you ever saw a kid liking rough things and becoming happy about it? Of course, not as kid always like shinny and smooth things. Do you ever saw a kid happy just sitting in a place which is like a cage? I know you haven't because kids like big and without an exception always want to chose an bigger and better version of any thing if you offer different version (obviously limit implied). Do you ever saw a kid without partial dependency or so-called loving somebody which is not about relation or it is some unconditional nonsense? Of course, no as so-called love is nothing more than partial dependency (it doesn't contradict interaction nor its a thing in itself), instead of that they want the best partially dependency and whosoever they maintain with they don't want any another person to maintain partial dependency with him/her (as it can decrease their partial dependency) which they show by their action quit profoundly. Do you ever saw a kid liking to be unhappy because of something and causing that because of delusion? Of course, not as they don't want to be in delusion i.e., thinking to be able to think about something which they can't think about and trying to take that.

At last the most important reason why kids are happy is because of the factor of new as every thing is new for them but also because there brain is developing very fast till age of 7 because of that they have lot of stimulation as I said earlier kids (if not born unfit) are default as they get and experienced of being thinker and normal without becoming one on there own because the brain has to develop - there is no other option, of course there can be more or less development which depends on the necessities. And needless to say, if kids don't get food or doesn't like it, they become crazy. But overall the most important thing is creativity which of course take all other prior factors in it that's why almost all the kids till age of 7 are overall very happy as there brain is creating it self for being better and all thinker and normal are overall happy as they are thinker/normal and default are progressive too i.e. happy as they cope up with the progress.

Chapter 8

Science Gets Retarded Because of Continuation of Different Fields of Philosophy

Let's start with the start, what is philosophy? I think answer to that you know now for sure even if you just read the title, philosophy is simply thoughts so any thinking which is nothing more than ideology is philosophy, so overall all any kind of retardness whether delusion, ignorance etc. is also philosophy. Obviously on the name of philosophy we do get some useful things but mostly people spread their bullshit or relative bullshit or relative ideology because any ideology is philosophy (as most of the people are retard). But then obviously an progressive thing to do, which progressive people always thought of doing is to differentiate what kind of thinking lead to progress and what retard progress so they can eliminate that, now a days that thinking is known as science, there is no doubt people try to create relative bullshit or relative which doesn't lead to progress on the name of science too whether it's by a so called scientist or just any renovated retard, but overall we already have successfully collected all the prior useful thing and still keep adding under the name of science, at last philosophy is not science.

Today we live in the world where we are so close to end of science (specially physics and chemistry - knowledge wise), as progress is limited both quality and quantity wise but still most of the population have no idea about how we do progress and have no role in progress or in maintaining it. Obviously because of current state of world still there is a such thing like philosophy and specially different filed of philosophy which are crazy retarding in themselves and not only that the very notion of different files of philosophy is crazy retarding, mostly the base of defining different philosophy is obviously just having different thoughts category which is obviously is an relative bullshit though there is such thing like different categorization of things (absolutely) but it has nothing to do with relative bullshit categorization of thoughts. Even though the philosophy name was continued till today but obviously for doing progress philosophy have change quiet a lot from categorization of thoughts to categorization of things which is eventually became the base of science.

There is no doubt there have been things which have been called part of philosophy which today is known as science but certainly still we have continuation of philosophy and especially different field of its which is retarding the progress (science). I think best example of that would be philosophy of nature or natural philosophy, as in science while taking about nature (generally tress, rocks etc.) we got things like gravity but than still there is an continuation of that philosophy like nature is more stimulating, relaxing, or have some relative bullshit even though we know today or in direct search for exactly what is what, how things interact and why they interact, so for example we know green colour is more stimulating because we have more receptors for green colour therefore nothing magical about tress, more space help us to relax and to be creative irrespective of any space, more oxygen to a limit is better, but than still there many nonsense which are continued on the name of that philosophy, like there is something known as unnatural, not organic, not pure which are obviously is an relative bullshit. A great example of that in today's biology would be continuation of relative bullshit methods of treatments on the name of homeopathy, Ayurveda, holy moly or witch magic etc., even thought it is quiet obvious there can be only one way of treatment i.e. knowing exactly what is what, how things interact, why they interact and how much of something is needed for what result and though today allopathy have been taken as an synonym to that kind of treatment. Virtually it can be called anything like 'cjcjdjkdc' if defined absolutely that's why name doesn't matter but what matter is there should not be any other way of treatment because there can't be any other knowledgeable real way.

Most of things in most of different philosophy branches and some branches of philosophy were just relative bullshit or relative or direct bullshit which have lead to no progress, some example of that would be philosophy of ethics, morals, politics, right, wrong, good, bad, evil, social, god, ghost and even science. Today there are many degrees and obviously any degree which is not about science is retardness, though some subjects have science in there name but are worthless and are not science like political science, moral science, social science, physiological

Science Gets Retarded Because of Continuation of Different Fields of Philosophy

science etc. The problem is quite obvious (if you are not retard), for example philosophy of science is purely retardness as what is knowledge which is obviously progressive is or would be taken as a part of science (progress is absolute) and what is not progressive or relative bullshit or bullshit or relative which lead to no progress would simply be discarded but still there is continuation of the philosophy of science obviously through which some renovated retard 'retard' the progress (science) insanely. Just to get an another example you can find renovated retards here and there shouting how some moral, ethics, political philosophy lead to progress but than it is quiet obvious progress of any thing is absolute so there can't be another way to do it so it obscured to say there can be different kind of progress and specially different things or way to do same progress of any particular thing, basically saying when things are exactly same but yet they are different or visa versa because of some relative bullshit or relative. Some people ask what is science to that some people answer is that science is a set of particular doings but science is simply anything or anything progressive because there is no such thing like unreal nor there is a such thing like doing progress with pure relative or relative bullshit or bullshit.

Note – The biggest problem on the name of education is defiantly wasting money on the name of degrees which are not science and trying to give or giving it to retards, but my major concern is the degrees which has basic science as their part - they are very hyped and contains information which is totally worthless even if it is not relative or relative bullshit or direct bullshit which overall increase the fees and especially the number of years. I would say if you are under 20 and graduated from any other subjects than PCM or PCB then definitely you should repeat 11th and 12th grade with them - if you want to learn science now, rather than doing this or that major or minor or whatever with bit of science involved.

Today most people have lots of there relative bullshit or relative or bullshit to call progressive and obviously the most of population is retard hence relative bullshit or relative are the most famous. For example, some renovated retard may say progress in any sector or any kind or of any people happened or happens because of some kind of political or social reform which is some relative bullshit or relative or direct bullshit which is obviously is not science. Example of above would be people saying a activist do so much of progress who fight of justice, equality, human rights and answer is obviously they retard the progress by talking about relative bullshit thing like that, though in between sometimes retards can get benefit of progress they never did nor have been an part of (which would be an unfair exchange), but obviously they don't become progressive and overall that is just more retardness. A famous activist example would be feminist (who are obviously retard), so what they do? Fight for the rights of females? What are rights? Something which should be done because it is right and why it is right because it should be done? So how much progress feminist have done? How many feminists are thinker or normal or even very lower end of default and why would any sane female would be feminist who has progressive things to do? So, what is females should get which they didn't got because of something like that? Equality, more wage, justice, etc.? Obviously, there can be unfair exchange which obviously retardness the progress but how other retard people without being progressive can do any progress for oneself or for others or overall. One may say because of the efforts of feminist who made social and political reform today's females are more in jobs, gets better wages etc. Without understanding what jobs are about, how more progress is done and what are the different processes are.

Obviously, the reality and progress have all to do with science and nothing to do with feminist or any so-called leader, god etc. I thinking talking about females is an great example of progress (science) as they are half of the variety of human being and highly talked about subject, for example one may say most of the female used to do and still do lot more than male (specially quantity wise) because they did or do home work because that is more physical work but yet they got less then male in every sense but obviously it is scientifically flawed as fit males are way better than fit female to do more physical work and if home work would be more in itself then male would have done that instead of females. From seeing the history why female mostly got less is because they were mostly doing less especially as most of progress (even till 1900) were crazy physical or bit some physical complication were involved and it is quiet obvious there were less females as defaults specially thinker and normal because of the very initial nature of progress for example progress for cave men would be trying to find a particular stone and carving it even if it means climbing hard mountains to find particular stone. It is quiet obvious there must have been female thinker or normal and defaults but obviously far less comparatively to male (percentage wise). I think an example of what progress could have been done by females which were technically less physical would be major amount of contribution in creation of speech and language as females can easily show more different precise facial expression specially because of there skin, they are bit more precise in preconisation of expression, they are more emotion hence can show more emotion easily and finally they have thin and small vocal cord compared to male which

Science Gets Retarded Because of Continuation of Different Fields of Philosophy

obviously helps them to speak faster, with less efforts and with more different tone than male (very easily).

At last, I will just say to progressive people don't role in the retardness of different field of philosophy ever in the field or domain in which they do progress -even a bit and because progress is so much today if you cope up with it then definitely it would be very difficult to role in nonsense. And I also want to say it always have been a rare thing that people got way less than (like a deviation of 100% or more) what they deserve (basically did and have known) but it's never have been a rare case people got way more than what they deserved.

Chapter 9

Justice Is Relative Bullshit

When it comes about talking crime retards go crazy, they start defining people as evil - very very harmful to society even though they them self is retard and off course they (majority) retard the progress. Tough there is no such thing like evil or good, every person does what he/she think is necessary to do but still there are laws, in which one get punished to do what he/she think is necessary to think or do. Who made the laws? Does Laws are really something useful? Answer to these question is, laws are made by renovated retard on the demand of retard, for the retard (which basically means they are relative bullshit) and only to be applied on the retards (mostly) and overall laws are not at all useful in any kind of progress and overall don't do any progress, though with passing time they make sure retards exist after all they are according to retards only to make sure there survival and there future generation survival but if something is retarding it lead to retardness only which means doom of retards by making them more retard.

What are the two biggest so-called crimes? I guess murder and rape, let's talk about them. First rape, so what is rape? Something done to a person which is he/she don't wanted sexually then if that the case it means doing something unnecessary to a person sexually but then in what term people define to do something unnecessary to a person, let's say there is male he is being raped by a female that means female is doing something unnecessary according to the male which he doesn't want but if that the case male body will not respond sexually to what so ever the female do because nobody's body respond to unnecessary thing then how come a female can rape a male? If male think it is unnecessary to get excited then male will not ejaculate don't mater whatsoever the female do and even will not release bulbourethral gland (Cowper's gland) secretion that simply means female is just rubbing the penis of that male how come it can be the one of the biggest crimes (even if crimes mean retardness at personal level)? And top of all if a male says a female raped him and she got pregnant then for sure that person is lying about rape and again how a person define rape that also something to think on and how many times this happens that male didn't get excited in between? If we talk about the female, then female also can't be excited if she thinks a male is doing something unnecessary to her and she will also not release the bulbourethral gland (Bartholin's gland) secretion but does that the case always, so-called raped women (proven by court or something) don't release any kind of secretion or never get excited in between? Again, that don't matter before the scenario or after the scenario whether a male or the female think it is necessary or not, it is about that moment what that male or female think is necessary? If in between so called rape if a male and female who is raped (allegedly) got excited then doesn't that person got the pleasure through that, does any body has done harm which is more bigger than every thing in this world or even at personal level, which has retarded the progress? (Specially whatsoever harmful happen to retards doesn't retard the progress instead can boast progress very much indirectly).

If you have a doubt that body don't respond to unnecessary thing then I have task for you from one hand you rub your vagina or do back and forth on penis and from one hand you do maths not too hard just two digit multiplication if you do continuous maths and that motion on your genital then you will realize that you have even not secreted bulbourethral gland secretion because it was unnecessary to get excited because you were doing maths so your focus is on math and motion (from which I mean as you are tingling your focus in between motion and maths) even though you are touching your penis or vagina you will not be excited and I expect this much from my readers because I am ambidextrous and I can write simultaneously two different word at the same time because my tinkling of focus is fast and even if you fail in doing that then I also have another things to prove that body don't do unnecessary things i.e. if a person take any hormone on regular basis for a long time his/her body will stop producing or will produce less it because it become unnecessary to do so and even after that person stop taking that his/her body will not produce it again if that person is doing this from long time as it must have caused a change in body and brain structure which can't be change by them self or certain thing, so if you want to try that you can take hormone and do the experiment.

If the concept of rape is so profound and well know then does it exist in other animals? Though as far as I know there is not such thing like rape law for other animal on something like a male dog has raped the female dog or visa versa and though there are research on excitement of female and progeny, according to which number of progeny is connected to excitement of female in some animal but researches like these I don't think is something to be considered to support something particular but still what about other animal if they just feel unnecessary to have sex and that time other animal do sex with it then how does it affect and if it's affect is related to progeny then should that process or that species would be whipped out by natural selection or see some serious consequences and does the nonsense on the name of rape lead to any progress? One fact which we can't ignore rape thing is more about female and at the same time many female have fantasy related to so-called rape (or basically they are delusion about what rape is) and why a person have fantasy if that person doesn't wanted it to fulfilled (most probably because females didn't got there prince charming as promised by there parents) and for sure people have sex fantasy (though there is no doubt that rape generally never happens or happened because of libido as per the record also). I do want to be clear about one thing if you are a fit male or female then for sure you will have libido to fit male or female who is beautiful irrespective of relative bullshit like marriage (relative), monogamy (relative) or overall knowledge about that person but it's a different thing you have sex or not.

Now as I told you we will talk about more stimulation, we will talk about that here as we are talking about people doing retarding things and talking nonsense, so we must know what stimulation is first (obviously about happiness) and how people lead to retardness on there own. Now here is the reasoning about fantasy, that to stimulation more senses together nothing more than that, so basically if a person have five fantasy then if he/she say he/she like this one the most then you will easily able to see that one going to be the stimulation of more senses together and that why it is impossible that a person don't have sex fantasy or any fantasy (if fit), if a person say so it means that person is denying from fulfilling necessities because thoughts are nothing more then necessities, and person can't feel sad if the person is on lot of stimulation and person who keep on stimulating his/her through many senses together at same time feel sad very rarely (obviously limits implied).

Now let me give you an example of more stimulation that is rainy season and when rain happens most of the people like that let me tell you why.
1. It stimulate many receptors of skin as wind blows and specially with moisture and moisture in air in itself and if you are under rain then it will stimulation almost every receptor of skin (categorically).

2. It comes with a noise which not chaotic as it is not so random which also stimulate the brain.
3. At the time of mild rain people like weather as it is no so bright and not so dull which also stimulate the brain uniformly.
4. Stimulation through smell because of secretion from plants and microbes.
5. Receptors of smells and taste doesn't have some connection or same receptors but they are intertwined in our whole perception about something (especially memory plays an important role), so smell start stimulating taste perception too and people prefer to eat something particular at raining time which again stimulate the brain (memory have quiet important role) and if all these stimulation and some other circumstances cause urge of romance or sex and a person do that then you can understand overall lots and lots of stimulation and that's why many people like talking shower for long time (may while doing other things).

If you feel sad or bored it is very easy to feel happy just stimulate all of the senses (limit implied and considering your are not unfit) at the same time but instead of that retard people who feel sad they show retardness, they cut more and more stimulation (or basically rolling in more nonsense which is not anything real hence no stimulation really) and after that try to have stimulation through something very particular which eventually they get addicted to (you can't addicted to any thing particular if you have overall lot stimulation and lot of different stimulation through lot of other things which is quite obvious and obviously you will not be depressed at the first place) and as I told you person use memory when there less stimulation so basically retard make sure to feel more and more miserable when they cut there stimulation and one must remember a person can't be addicted to drugs or alcohol or whatever if he/she gets lot of stimulation without them beforehand. Stimulation of senses can help in many thing to have more stimulation for better experience for example if you are learning something stimulate all of you sense to learn better sit where wind blow constantly, move your body which involve reflex so your focus don't go in moving too much but still stimulate the brain, eat something particular every time you learn but should be of one taste only so it don't take your focus away like chuingum, use one particular smell again not too many different smell so that it don't take your focus away etc.

Now back to the topic, now if we talk about child abuse or you can say child rape or something like that then it is well known surveys figure that at least 90% of child abuse are done by a known person of that child only that simply means child was shit (retard) that's the only way a person can't differentiate between retardness and progress. That obvious too now a days kids (not all obviously but most) have become more retard the then ever (specially considering we have more progress than ever), they need safe zones in school so they can hide from other kids of there own age group, if a kid can't tackle his/her own age group kids I don't know on what basis that kid is fit to survive (and giving benefits of the progress to retards make retards more retard) and it is very obvious that without facing the thing no solution can be created and without being in a situation person can't be creative to do more or new (without consideration of something you can't work on that), to be creative - person have to be in situation, think on your own can a bird know it will fly or not in first attempt (if born fit) without jumping out of nest, when a bird jump from the nest for the first time believing that it has wing and it will work and it will fly even if that time it's wing doesn't work with proper motion at least it got to know what can be done more properly to make it work (if bird will be absolutist it will not believe either way baselessly, it will just consider what it can that is it got wing or not i.e. born fit or not and a situation in which they have to do something on there own). If a human being is not born unfit then definitely what another equally fit human can do, he/she can do that too but obviously if that person just become retard i.e., doesn't coping up with the progress even though he/she could have (i.e., born fit) then obviously then that person would become unfit eventually and not only that while becoming unfit that person will become more retard and hence more miserable and overall worthless for progress.

One thing I want to say about the bird and about you to you that even if you brain doesn't work when you or bird thought it would still it is better to die worthlessly today while trying to do something (basically rolling in relative bullshit or relative or direct bullshit) then to live worthlessly and then die worthlessly but now in schools they give trophy to many people making everybody believe (delusion) that has done a great thing in this and that form, though most recently that thing is now replaced by another thing which is giving participation certificate (some time even at the time of participation only before the thing get's over) in this scenario all retard who have done nothing also get the feeling of doing something or in language of retards - being a part of something big (bullshit), what a joke. Another thing, schools which gives more relative or relative bullshit option (like moral science, cooking, social activities- specially debates, community service, religion, culture, sports, arts, political science, general knowledge, history of retardness, retarding stories on the name of literature, different literature) which are just completely worth less to follow, in reality they are schools which are called the best schools, so I told you it is very easy to become a renovated retard just do think in term of making thing relative or relative bullshit. Giving retards the benefit of progress is just retardness.

Wait, I forget about the most important thing which schools teaches that is how to be a sticky retard, how to follow the pattern and how to be passionate! Which obviously comprises with one of the biggest relative bullshit i.e. this person brain (if born fit) is not made for science but it can be better at something else like above things (we talked about) and those can also bit useful for something or any kind of progress, let me tell you the best way to get A grades in school and college life is just follow small little dangling pattern and let me tell a way for never creating new things and being a retard just follow small little dangling patters (obvious while not really understanding things) all of which will break one day and you will shown that you were just folling around. As I already told you it depends on the person whether that person want to become a retard, thinker, normal or renovated retard but there are things which make retard more retard and that much hard wired that it become hard to change in thinker, normal or default, after all a person don't have whole life to change.

Again back to the child abuse thing I don't know why survey don't say 100% so called abuse done by known person but thing is clear whether it is rape or child abuse it can be only happen when a person himself/herself is retard too because nobody do the unnecessary thing to any body and to do something to someone that person should in his/her circumstance before hand (and not just superficially). Does any body in whole world is roaming here and there to just rape people Or to just to kill people? Does anybody rape anybody? Does anybody kill anybody? A person can't kill a person until and unless that is necessary for that person to do so and it is well known fact the people who are psychopath have problem in there brain structure whether it's the hype of so called smaller amygdala or less sensitive amygdala or anything less and look generally same species doesn't attack each other because they have same basic necessities which includes they have almost same brain structure and body structure (generally those things are important to become better competitor together) and person who act like crazy also have some kind of different brain structure problem. I want to ask does before the trail of every case does brain scan happen? The people who know the person who has done so called crime before hand does that people are not shit (retard) too? Off course shit and shit know each other and if a person know before hand one particular group or area is shit why that person don't rise from there and do something worthwhile, if that person who got rape or so is not retard why that person say after some kind of incident that they fooled me or something like this, doesn't it is an simple logic if you are fool then only you can be fooled like crazy? And there is no doubt fooling is nothing more than taking relative or relative bullshit mostly (though people get fooled by direct bullshit too) and if a person doesn't show retardness how that person can come into any kind of relative talk. There is no doubt in that you can't accept or reject something without considering it and you can't consider something if there is no option of consideration.

Now if we talk about particulars laws for rape, murder or whatever does that laws are made by doctor or by thinkers on the bases of some knowledge and progress? Off course not. On what basis degree of crime is measured if laws are made by renovated retard who don't know even a bit about anything or any progress overall and that too on the demand of retard who are worthless for progress (retard) them self. Top of why not all judges should always proof that he/she is above the person under evaluation or not both mentally and physically (especially for particular things) so that he/she can understand the case at the first place (and why we should waste money on retards through so called justice system)? Off course there can be no justice be made (to make nonsense scenically any way progressive) as every body do what he or she think it is necessary to do but off course there is always some thing which lead to progress and some thing which retard progress but laws are not made exclusively for maintaining progress but for sure is mostly relative or relative bullshit.

Every thought is one and the same and the result of necessities then how come a person can differentiate between any thoughts or any crime and every crime is relative bullshit as what people define it by, but still misery is result of retardness and it happens because people are retard, they think in terms of relativity or bullshit, then don't you think being a retard is the biggest crime (if we define it by retardness which led to misery at personal or overall level) as all retardness and all worst retarding nonsense origin from retards? Most importantly all crime starts and all nonsense or creator of them rise from highly populated areas so having more kid than a person can handle is not the biggest crime? And on what bases a law can put a person in a jail(cage) even though there is nothing like bad and wrong exist, how one can justify that as justice doesn't exist? Though one can make borders in between people (but why retards should exist at the first place) or kill people so that particular person don't interact with other group of people, for instance making boundaries can be an solution of solving retardness (but only for young, so that they don't become more retard) and that can be practiced as some short of open jail (not cage) and for sure caging a person for some period of time makes no sense and make no difference as they do the same thing when they come out because there necessities are not changed they remain the same as they were before and if they do the same thing again caging them again is not useful but just wastage of money, there is no doubt in that the people who are put in open jail kind of thing and work is done on changing there necessities generally don't do the same thing again (most probably because they have become less retard not default but less is less) instead of that people who are caged do the same thing again and you can check thing or records on your own, though it is obvious why. But right now, we are way overpopulated so any retard should be killed for slight bit of retardness which has come to focus.

In any scenario killing person is not justified (by which I mean not progressive) if person is thinker or normal whether that person has killed somebody or raped somebody, especially when so-called victim was a retard (instead of that retard and other retard should be dead or at least their benefits should be cut off). If a person is under 30 (retard) and we are underpopulated so much so more progress can't be done then person should not be killed as that person can still change (if possible) but obviously a person can't retard things significantly at present just because that person can cope up with the progress in future (though we are crazy overpopulated so retards should be killed at any mistake and lot of money shouldn't be spent on name of justice on retards) and in an ideal world where is no retard before hand then a person who become retard would be whip out immediately so obviously to whip out retard people we should make sure there is no option to survive as a retard. There is no doubt in that laws are one of the biggest pile of relative, bullshit and relatives bullshit ever created by renovated retards and retards after mythologies (which kind of have lot of rules and laws in itself) and there is no doubt in that more and more laws are made on the demand of retard (without having an restriction like if you create one more law then you have to remove two prior laws) which retard the progress and lead to nowhere for instance let's take laws on so called verbal abuse, there is no doubt in that there no such thing can exist like verbal abuse because words are nothing more than bunch of terms to refer to certain things and it is relative bullshit (really for most person as doesn't really think all the way through), if people are highly driven towards the relative thing that means people are retards nothing more than that, now the result of these laws people have become more and more retard and there some quiet funny stuff happen these days like they do suicide if they don't get likes on social media, they feel sad if somebody dislike them virtually, they start feeling shit (which basically most of the people are indeed but only sometime they really accept that) and if somebody dislike them in front of other people they will pass away at the moment, people can't disagree now a days directly on the face they disagree virtually what a joke (which give more scope of creating relative or relative bullshit), people can't talk face to face they text, most people want other people to do stuff and watch them which they them self want (wanting more pseudo experience) and specially want to have all direct benefits of the progress which they never did.

One of biggest recent relative bullshit is people's mental health related laws, it is basically about the hype of things like depression. I want to be clear about one thing there is not such thing like a sudden inducement of something with words or something which is not an direct inducement i.e. not really an inducement which causes chemical or hormonal imbalance or damage and any kind of hormonal or chemical imbalance in the body on it's own takes lot of time, for sure not one moment or a day thing. Now days people talk about some sort of mental damage (relative bullshit) even though there is no damage at brain and no chemical imbalance, quiet frankly no body can do metal damage to anybody directly without directly hitting them or introducing something to there body. It not an new thing laws are crazy retarding, for example a person who killed a person and says that he was instructed by god or ghost (obviously crazy) would get lot's of medical facility instead of death penalty as that is obviously an lost call for any kind of progress (don't forget we are over populated too) but a person who overall cope up with bit of progress and kills a person (or more) who are for sure worthless for any kind of progress would get an death penalty if that person's directly tell the reason why he/she did so (though that's why progressive person would not directly kill retards for showing retardness at first place which is not progressive but retarding). Obviously, the biggest relative bullshit of laws is everybody is equal and laws or something should be equal for everybody.

Now updating this book 2020 now there are more laws are in making like making a law which I call the fat law according to which calling someone fat is hate crime now that's how you cross all limit of retardness because nobody would call a fit person 'fat' to really mean it nor it would mean anything or refer to anything, a person would only call a fat person 'fat' to mean it so basically saying reality is crime though it is not something new you can't call a retard 'retard' because it is also hate crime so basically you can't say the reality because it comes under crime, basically being progressive which is a result of being better (for sure being fit) is retardness and removing retardness is also retardness some how or at least that's what laws meant by it or at least that's what people living who have delusion of retardness to be progressive and leading to happiness is ok with (there is no doubt retards should not get benefit of the progress which they never did nor ever cop up with as it retard progress and there is absolutely no retardness in hating retards and making sure they get wiped out.) And there is no doubt how unfit these crazy fat people are for survival though now corona must have proved this and there is no doubt in that major cause of death is heart failure and need less to say fat ass have cardio vascular problems (of course they are unfit) and just for information more than 40% population is crazy fat and 60% population have health problems which are considerable in terms of whether person is fit or not physically and mentally, and only less than 5% population has no health problem in any way (remember only less than 5% kids are born purely unfit). One very simple thing what is unfit looks ugly. Updating once again just before publishing today I got to know even showing fat ass literally is a crime though it is obvious why because fat ass looks ugly and shit know they look ugly so of course there is need of law like that. One more thing I don't want majority to like me as I want them to hate me as that will happen if I am talking progressive (absolute). PS – There came be some renovated retards who don't want certain nonsense to exist because of other certain nonsense but doesn't mean they are not retarding and this is quiet common way to get more famous while trying to act like useful which obviously retards would like believe.

After sometime there going to be some more new retard laws which I would call a tone law and body law in which if person talk in harsh tone even without using so called bad words then also it will be a hate crime and if somebody (specially to retard) just show strong body posture to somebody (specially to retard) it will also count as hate crime (though today only showing a middle finger or any other bullshit posture to judge or government official is a big crime, though it not explained by laws how hating a retard is retardness, oh I forgot laws are not made just for progress but made mostly for retardness), who are judges and government official anyway? off course renovated retards and I have no idea how person who created nothing new, modified nothing, don't cope up with progress can understand everything, though generally only retard and renovated have to face retards and renovated retards. After all these laws guess what going to be happen next? Off course all this nonsense would be whipped out with these retards. One must remember shit (retardness of any kind) only happen to shit because shit interact with shit and nothing can happen without interaction as no necessities can't be formed about something particular without interaction with that particular thing. I told you before hand if you are shit then surround yourself with thinker, normal and default to become a default (by interaction and learning knowledge and that will make sure retards don't surround you, only if your willing to) but these retards have retard parents or surround them self with other retards or renovated retards who make retard more retard by telling things like judge a person by relative bullshit instead of judging a person by what he/she has created and know, they tell so because they them self are worthless piece for any progress and created nothing, if you want to change and hard time changing then look who you eat with, sit with, talk with, think of and do work with, do they have created anything in reality or cope up with any progress?

Nobody is evil or good person, people do thing according to there necessities then we should think of chancing people necessities (if possible) as I told you earlier we all are not born as biased and crazy to role in relative or relative bullshit or bullshit, nobody was born with something nor bounded to follow something particular but still most chose to be religious about particular god, ghost, rule, regulation or any other nonsense concept. Laws (by which I mean retards should get whipped out and there should be no option to become retard) should be made to make sure people don't become religious which means not making people follow something but stopping people to be religious as there is no doubt in that more happy country overall (country where thinker/normal and defaults population is more than 40%) have less religious people it is not like being religious make people retard but retard people become religious and more retard through that, laws should be made to protect people from particular ideology not to protect particular ideology (till we achieve ultimate progress at least quality wise).

Quiet frankly there is no need of laws if nobody wants to show any retardness and very minimal need of laws if there is no retard overall. By this in no way I mean that we should not create things which are progressive for example in the case of roads and vehicles - creating traffic lights, positioning speed limitless in better ways, better roads with better equipped safety, making roads seems visually particular narrower or wider whenever necessary etc. Though today most of the laws are not for progress, the basic idea of law is not progressive, especially laws are relative bullshit complex for seizing more power and money. The things which we need is infrastructure, competition and making sure there is no money going to retards and their systems, as if ultimate progress is achieved retarding system can't exist and even when we are close to ultimate progress still retarding systems can't exist for long terms compared to progressive system at that period if there is no continuous supply of at least the same amount of money from outside to that system, best and biggest example of that are governments (retarding systems).

And at last, one must remember that even the species who show cannibalism show cannibalism only when there is necessity to do so not every time so saying any way, they just do this or that, or this or that should be done or should not be done because it is good or bad or illegal or legal or whatever is very retarding. I think the most important thing is 'renovated retard' retard the progress the most because they got the creation of thinker and normal because of retards and have excess to every thing. Look even a retard kill somebody on that basis that some renovated retard told him/her to do so as it is good which is relative bullshit in itself as why it should be done just because it is good? Then why it is good just because it should be done? Still, it would not be as unnecessary thing to do as that person doesn't understand why to do but that person understand what to and do that because that person is a retard who suffers from the delusion (we have to be clear about what lead progress and what retards it and we should not have relative or relative bullshit laws like if somebody killed some this should be done). Motive of the whole chapter is justice doesn't exist and what people say or do on the name of that is nonsense and very retarding because things are the way they are, they can be changed if possible but one can't do anything for what they have been other then getting rid of retardness. I think if you ask your self what is crime? Then I think you not going to have an absolute definition but I think absolute crime (if we want to define that) is the one which hinder the progress or hindering the person who led progress or cope up with it, so in turn hindering the progress. In this way most of the population are criminals and the best thing is to do is kill all criminals. And what is justice? I don't know what you mean by that but I can't think of better thing than progress in it self for progress and for making people happy and obviously whipping out all retards.

Chapter 10

Equality Is Nonsense

First tell me who talk about equality here and there? Off course retard and renovated retard, why they talk about it? Because they are retards and want more things nothing more than that, again it is a relative thing (at least) which doesn't exist at the first place things are what they are nor equal nor unequal (in any relative sense) every different thing is just different, retards use this so called equality thing so they get things from thinkers, normal and defaults without doing any thing or while doing the least possible and on what basis retard think that thinkers and normal owe them something? nobody knows (as they just think that on bases of relative bullshit or relative which is baseless i.e. an delusion). They them self don't create any thing and then they say why they don't have this or that and why they don't have power of exchanging goods. And who promote equality? Renovated retard, who them self has created nothing and when in old time these renovated retards were use to promote equality either they used to have slaves them self or they use to be nothing more than shitty leader who talk relative bullshit and who is nothing on his/her own, just popular figure who talk relative bullshit (mostly), off course that's why they were popular at the first place (just an important remark it's better to slave retards i.e., majority right now). Most importantly retards have excuses like they don't have technology to do the progress- what a joke, first progress for personal level means whatsoever your are doing you find a way on your own to do it in a better ways and with more efficiency with less effort and with less human resources but retards are retard at personal level too because they don't do any kind of progress and retard the progress (definitely getting benefit of the progress one didn't did or cope up with will never be progressive and definitely retards asking for benefit of the progress because other retard have got that is not more progress but more retardness).

For example, ask a retard how you will use a stream of water passing by, let say the work of retard is to break stone then retard will reply it is impossible to use it to break stone and that's why that retard is 'retard'. There is no doubt in that every body (thinker/normal and defaults) should access to new technology so they can modify it for better and understand the level so they can think of what next level can be or what they have created is new or not, if new then - how and how useful. But right now, lot of people have excess to internet at least 4.5 billion people, what they do with it? Either use social media for fulfilling there craving of nonsense or use the search engines for fulfilling there craving for nonsense and that's why relative thing dominate all over internet (though I am not saying internet is filled with knowledge and it's quiet obvious why). Even though a person lives where services are not present then still option of running away is always there.

At this point I want you to understand equality doesn't exist as nothing is equal for different thing to be equal, they have to be relative bullshit or relative and I already told you why nothing is relative, there can be same thing here and there in between but not equal if you want to call same thing equal it is not ok. One can make a point like all of us are human being so we are equal, I want you to understand that this doesn't prove any thing as something in common or same in between two different thing doesn't make thing equal for example even though all of us chordates that doesn't mean all chordates are equal, we are put under chordates on the basis of the same thing we got (at least at embryonic stage) 1. Post anal tail 2. Phalangeal gill slits 3. Notochord 4. Nerve chord. Not that all cordate are equal, if it question of definition of species then is defined on the basis of sexual intercourse then also a thinker and normal (basically the better ones) would not prefer to do sex with a retard specially to have offspring (which a well know phenomena in any species - best want best) and top of all human being are most creative species but if person is a retard and can't come up with something on his or her own but just can copy menial thing, how that being would not be consider as most creating being who is an retard as not being to cope up with same species progress and retard progress? Equal is just impossible.

Let's talk bit about slavery and eradicate most of it's nonsense and lies on the name of facts-

1. Relative of owners or slaves – It's starts like a pretty common well know way like Americans enslave the Africans etc. First, I want to be clear about the fact that most of the world population before 1800's used to live in the condition which

less than 15% of world population live in today, so owing a slave is quiet a far cry for major. And every country had slaves and having slave from another country far away was not even in somebodies thinking before medieval period.

2. Born slave or child slave – People say there is no fault of a person in being born slave so they should not be slaved. First if you are born retard than for sure it's your fault because that's what you are. Second it's a lie people use to born slave as quiet frankly it's very retarding to own a child and even to account for your slave child. Not only that mostly slave were the adults who are forced to do work by certain people by certain standards, so basically most of the slaves were not slave by birth or become slave the moment they turned adult but were moving freely as to say but obviously not well off compared to slaved people.

3. Slave were not well off with the master than what they were before – Mostly answer to that is no because of very simple reason most of the population have been retard and there was simply not enough money which has everything to do with level of progress (though today something different is happening). Another popular myth in that is slaves' families were used to get destroyed by masters, answer is obviously no - being slaves gives the financially stability which otherwise most of the retards doesn't use to have and master were not keen or fan of destroying families of slaves, obviously. One more thing being a slave can give more exposure to different stuff.

4. All slaves were the same – Answer is absolutely no, as first – there were slave at different place holding different position and possession, second - most of the slave were menial and never learned anything after being slave but some use to, who use to work like or less than 9-5 jobs and make master lot's of money and hence they also use to get significant money through which they pay of there slavery and live well off than majority.

5. Slave use to work for more than 10 or 12 hours per day- That's impossible even if somebody want that's to happen because of many reasons, most important reason before 1900's was sunrise and sunset is the most important thing. There are people today who work 10-12 hour a day specially some crazy physical or mental work! - obviously it's a myth too as there is not even a single person like that nor a single company which employ people like that exist because of many reasons including there is no reason to do so for any kind profit nor really can be done if company want to profitable specially with stability and all this has nothing to do with shitty laws. Ps – there never have been a single person working 10-12

hour per day nor ever there will be and obviously working job is about certain things.

6. Slave use to work only for master- obviously answer is no, as they don't usually use to work from sunrise to sunset for master nor work every day for master, so in meanwhile they may work on something else.

7. Slavery was about race – Obviously this a very retarding statement to make because of many reasons, first – there are lots of relative or relative bullshit or direct bullshit which people can't clear because mostly they are crazy retard, second race can't be defined today with the real bases which it use to have for example, because of less progress there were not lot of different work and as most of population always have being retard most people doesn't use to do even bit different from there parent and ancestors for centuries, today either people (majority) simply not doing anything really which make them cope up with progress but yet gets lot's of benefit of progress and there are people who are simply coping up with progress which is very high and we are close to ultimate progress at least quality wise. Mostly when it is a talk of slave about race obviously it is because retard want more stuff, one of the genius reasoning of retards is look that retard got benefit of the progress I should have that too. And people who say slavery is about race look because mostly in America they had African slave, so African is a race specially of less white people so it is about race, answer is absolutely no, though it does shows flawed accountability of people.

One important thing to understand is having a preference is not retarding in it self but will be if it is about retarding things and to be clear about thing I can tell you my preference and not preference at all for example I prefer more white female and not all prefer very less white female (so called chocolate colour) for relationship or any other interaction connected to that kind specially because of three reasons, first- more white is more stimulating, second – I am use to more white females (interaction of A and B depends on A and B for sure at least, both of which can change), third – I am more white because of which I and others can always make direct comparison very easily which we talked about before. But that no way means I will not work with a very less white female or male who is progressive as I am not a retard and obviously, I don't make some relative or relative bullshit. And just because you prefer something that doesn't mean you doesn't prefer something else and definitely there is a such thing like more or less preferred or not preferred at all which can be very progressive.

8. Master owe something to slave – Obviously answer is no, as I said before people who use to become slave there were not well off nor they mostly become slave in early their life which means they were retard any way which doesn't lead to progress and it can't make sense in any way that if my parents or ancestor were slave then their master or master family owe me something. And anybody who makes a profit by doing progressive thing then that person owe nothing to any person but other people owe that person specially in today's world. Nobody can't be robed by somebody, who doesn't had anything before hand they can only be made slave.

9. Slavery got demolished by political or social reforms – First there is no such thing like social and political reform, second - slavery got demolished because of lot of people getting benefit of progress (including retards) and that's why by the west first (contradictory to popular myths) but that doesn't mean demolition of slavery was progressive as the only reason that become possible was by taking more mostly simply by taking at least the same amount out of GDP again and again (though that percentage from some decades has risen very significantly which is crazy retarding) which was not a new thing but that percentage got increased also and as there were more money and more percentage of money more retard people survived but also got of very less miserable condition the result of that is we are overpopulated, most of population doesn't work at real full time or part-time job and at best knowledge of majority doesn't surpass the knowledge of scientists at 1700's.

10. Demolition of slavery is a sign of progress – It could have been, as if we would have achieved ultimate progress - living like a retard would be impossible and there would be ultimate quantity and quality, in which overpopulation is impossible and there would be the best atomization. One important thing to understand when slavery was getting demolished enslaving has been quiet less profitable or was becoming quiet retarding for the owners (not overall) especially because of two reasons job dilation (as more slave here hired) and slave were becoming more retard or worthless (especially because there was more progress).

11. Lie of generational wealth – This one definitely got quiet some baggage so I will simply ask you some question, how many businesses (big or small) you know which are running from centuries? Do we have way more money than 1700's or not? Do we have more field of work or not? Do we have more knowledge or not? Did we have done more progress or not? Are we overall progressive or not? Are most of the rich retards or renovated retards?

12. What if I take your kid and make him/her slave? – I will say it depends, what I say for it is as if I some how have an unfit kid - I say totally take it, if I have a kid who become retard then first I will abandoned him/her anyway and then what you do to him or her is not my concern, other than that when ultimate progress is achieved a retard would not survive anyway. And again some thing same or in common doesn't make things equal, my kid is mine and your is yours and specially relative bullshit on the name of biological relation is not new for example how you can't have relationship with your mother or father as they are your parents or all parents like or love there kid and visa versa, ya like definition of parents and relationships can be relative bullshit but yet can mean something.

13. Hey I got a definition for you – So what? Even if people have a real absolute definition like that of slavery (now a days so called modern slavery) then they still make relative or relative bullshit out of it for example slavery should be demolished because it is bad, unethical, unmoral etc. Or we are equal so slavery should not be there or all the above points and below point.

14. Live and let live – Saying like that is a direct accountability flaw and that's why I don't wonder why it is so famous. But obviously that flaw stand in between progress specially after certain level of progress, for us which happened around medieval period and when people got very useful ships. Obviously, earth has a carrying capacity, population is way above that and majority is retard.

For the retards who believe in dividing thing equally then let say all the money get's divided equally in between all the population right now (which means everything and which is there at the first place because thinker, normal and defaults exist and existed, don't forget most of the population is retard), then let me tell you not only progress will be stop but all the production of goods and services will be stopped too as nobody would have that much to produce any goods or service (basically it also going to create decision making problem even if we consider no body is retard) and even we do this equal division at 4 billions population then also there will no production of goods and service, even at less than 1 billion we do this production will be very low, only some where way below 1 billion there can be an adequate production of good and services (considering all the people have an idea about how some particular work is done, and obviously just because some body got a million in currency doesn't mean that person can buy the particular stuff he/she want as you can't buy something when there is no seller and visa versa, and also because somebody have to hold the companies or commercial parts in share or whatever) but then also there would be people who would thinker and normal or defaults or retards or better progressive or more retarding and some people would perform better then others again there would be unequal distribution once again which will keep increasing which is progressive (which you can say shouldn't happen if you are an retard).

Just in case you have no idea how much more infrastructure (excluding any other goods) we need so that everybody has something to work with or work for couple of decades, it would equivalent to what we created from 1500's (not considering the fact that we don't have that much space, material for all that and it would not be progressive). Top of all this, this scenario of so much big population arises at the first place because retard and especially unfit survived and then they produced lot of kids who are also turned out to retard and especially become unfit so that they can have more of them in number so that then can make pressure on think and normal through renovated retard for more goods and services for so-called free and freedom.

Just in case you think rich pay less taxes then let me tell you are a retard, they pay more taxes as for example in a country if 20 % people controlled 60% money then there share in overall tax accumulated would be more than 60% that happen because taxes exemption for poor and lower middle class little by little adds and become very considerable and obviously if rich would be paying less this much big retards population would not there at the first place (I think at least you understand the difference in calculating per capita on average verses really calculating the whole thing). Though in above scenario taxes paid by rich should be less than 40% of tax accumulated (right now) as there money is more important and is leading to more progress (overall tax accumulated should be less by 20% at least at any country for equal contribution), not only that basically in any country the top 40% gets way less in return compared to what they have given in name of taxes and below 40% gets way more compared to what they have given in taxes (if any) which is just crazy retardness and is a retarding system (In almost every country below 40% doesn't pay any income tax at country level). It is just crazy retardness to impose more percentage of taxes on the very people who made overall progress, increased opportunities and increase overall money in the system (though there is myth lower middles and poor create opportunities for them self by having buying power, it's just like saying thing can be there without thinker or normal). I don't understand why there are benefits for the poor in the name of one day every body will have it all which obviously impossible (and even we can create more wealth or have more why we should give to retards specially when we are way over populated and majority is very retarding – more than ever, though that's the reason because of which we are overpopulated) and obviously those things retard the progress as it for sure make retard survive.

Now lets talk about so-called inequality with men and women, now you will see retard people here and there saying make things equal - women should get equal status, equal opportunities and bla bla bla , first let me tell you there no such thing like equality exist because male and female are not equal, this whole relative bullshit was created by retards only and something or things like this was never a concern in between thinkers and normal, it is very obvious any progressive person can rise from any where. But how this started? let me tell you how this all started, when retard men become more and more retard and worthless but still survived because they got the benefit of the progress they never did hence there become a shortage of people to do the labour work (not number wise) and menial things and these existed till today at the first place because retard people exist and never think of doing process and creating something which reduce there work while increasing efficiency and productivity, but to fulfil this whole a new pseudo shortage and the hype of thing like IT, education, etc. they starred saying women should be in equal number in jobs, let me tell you women can't take same amount of physical and mental stress as the women body is less toned to do physical work and mentally they become more emotional under so-called pressure (as they say) which you can check by studies and certainly having hype is not progressive (most jobs in the world is about menial work, hype or direct bullshit only but still a same menial work compared to earlier is less physical today with less working hour hence more female can do the same thing which you can see in some country number of female working is more or equal, don't forget female and male population is almost equal in the world right now) and obviously you shouldn't pay equal for unequal work. But still today many women are forced to do these thing (which you can say if you are retard but in reality it is the result of combined retardness of retards including females) because what progress we have today we could have it 21 century ago also, and overall impact of crazy retardness is fertility rate dropped after all this is a nonsense and retardness created by retards and there is no other reason behind fertility rate dropped so much last three decades and so as I said retards are 'retard', talk bullshit or relative or relative bullshit and show retardness and finally make sure there own doom, once and for all, the end of retardness (this century).

There is no doubt in that it is just an myth or nonsense that men hasn't treated women properly (which in itself an relative bullshit statement), this kind of thing only used to happen in between retards and renovated retard, and women do more physical work than men was also an old myth but now you can say that it is some what trying to become reality (at least quiet significantly more than ever) and result of reality in front of every one. According to most of the retard people something has changed women are at more better conditions and bla bla bla, at old time cavemen use to drag women by hair (which I don't known on what piece of evidence people say that and how they consider it as bad and what exactly they consider as bad), top of all something better has happened is also base less bullshit (considering majority is more retard then ever), the only thing happened is more women doing jobs (most of the jobs are menial) and most women are miserable (though less then ever because they got benefit of the progress which they never did or cope up with), according to some surveys 10-14% people cry once a week at there jobs and it not because job is there misery which they doesn't like or jobs are the problem - it is just that they are just retard and suffering from misery because of there own retardness, average working hours are not more than 6 hours a day whether it is 9-5 job or 9-7 job or something else which 30 years ago was 7½ or more (though it is totally an different thing that most of people in full time job can do the same work in 3-4 hour) but people are more retard (especially because of more progress) and more retards exist now, top of all average usage of phone or any device by under 35 going to touch 6 hours in 2 or 3 years which means they are more miserable and more retarding jobs are there because of which pays are less and that obvious why, but the most important thing which I want to tell you that up to 70% of menial work and labour work can be done by technology right now and I am not talking about some futuristic bullshit fairy tale technology, I am talking about what we currently have the only thing is it is still is not in use properly or more production is not there because people want jobs and off course retards retard the progress (and obviously we are way overpopulated).

One thing to very clear about is that we even don't need more default in world for progress and even if everybody becomes default by witch magic or you say it's the case (as it can't happen) still most of the population will live and dies miserably as we have this much population at the first place because there are many options to live as a retard. Right now, only less 25% of the people do real full-time jobs (not necessarily useful) and less 30% of the population do really full-time or part-time jobs (and obviously if you are a person who says that've# person work for 8 hour per day for 2 day a week so that person is full time employed or you say there are 3 people like that who work in same way then 3 people are employed instead of 1 than you are an idiot). And full-time jobs are not with same working hour and not with the same efficiency, at least what can be done by 2 is split between 3 in most of the jobs (one very important thing to remember job dilation decreases efficiency, accountability and productivity not only for the system but also for the personal level which overall lead to less better default personally and less default people). One of the famous bullshits or relative bullshit of equality is thing should start with equal education to all. let's say by witch magic education make every body default still we doesn't need that many defaults (and specially considering the reality i.e. more than 50% of the population is either graduated or graduating from high school still most of the population have no idea about basic science not even mid school level/course science). Some renovated retard educator out there clamming to teach for less or for free (obviously nothing can be free as their is just unfair exchange which obviously retard the progress), to them I simply want to ask are you increasing the number of seats in an collage or university for real, useful degree? Are you changing the exam pattern? Are you overall increasing the earth? Are you doing progress even? Did you come with something new or modified something?

I will end the topic of jobs by eradicating one of the biggest myth i.e. dirt poor people work the most in terms of quantity or working hours and obviously the reality is the upper middles class in any country are the people who work the most in terms of quantity or working hours (in any country there is a very significant rise in both quantity and quality in terms of output from lower middles class to upper middles class), the last 15% of the world population is the total worthless ones and doesn't have any real part-time or full time jobs (if you ever evaluate a slum you must be knowing how they don't do anything nor want to do anything which can lead to any kind of progress, needless to say only retards use the terms like working hard).

Another thing just for information most of world population is miserable which you can check from here and there survey but if you ask me how much I would say up to 85% as this is the percentage of retards and renovated retards, how we know it? It is very easy to know, we doesn't have more than 1 million products in terms of variety and even if 1000 people per product makings in a day, then also it makes just 1 billion and population going to 8 billion in 3 to 5 years (it crossed 8 billion at start of 2023) and not more than 120 billion people ever walked on this earth so how this remaining so much big population can be creative, productive and useful and if they would be- progress would over in a decade (remember progress is not limit less).

Back to the topic of women, there is no doubt in that a woman can be better thinkers than a man because being a thinker has nothing to do with being male or female for a particular thing (though very nature of something allows for more male thinker and normal) but just like most of the men are retard most of the women are retard too and shit happens to shit (overall retardness), but if you under 30 and want to change from retard to thinker or normal or default then first you must not opt for crazy physical jobs if any exist anymore and think of more about governing things (you know) while creating things that's only thing women should think of doing for menial jobs (though remember doing something is better than nothing). I already talk about thinkers before hand and most important if you are married and your husband will be retard too which has high probability as you were a retard and if he doesn't accept his retardness then give divorce (same is for male too) and don't have kids before 30 because it retard the brain structure directly and indirectly specially if you are retard (not necessary permanent change but defiantly you can become permanent retard). And again, not being more retard is very easy just don't be in the trap of relative or relative bullshit like equality.

The damaged cause by equality doesn't end there another retarding which equality has caused is survival of sexually unfit males and females who totality worth for progress anyway also, for example existence of people with crazy hormonal problem as most people are unfit physically, for example lots of males are sexually very less fit or unfit because of low testosterone level, less sperm count or any other retarding thing must have been whipped by overall current progress at any given period compared to the progressive systems as people who are successful overall (sexually) generally don't have low testosterone and less sperm count (though there is no direct proportional relation of testosterone and sperm count nor we know any perfect direct relation whether it is with FSH,LH,ADEH or something else but generally people with high testosterone and with no other hormone problem don't have low sperm count) but these people who have low testosterone exist today which you can easy see by comparing a photo or video of a men before 1950 and so called guys people on YouTube and social media, and because of which difference between male and female seem more faded to retards - result of which gender dysphoria kind of scam popup and there hype start after 1950, again as I told you people go more retard more scam go at hype just like global warming problem, co2 pollution, personal development, self help, motivation etc.

There is no doubt in that transgender are not real in the sense it is just relative bullshit of male and female rather they are just mentally retard people who create that relative bullshit and they are or becoming sexually unfit (and become more unfit) specially driven by blockers, intake of hormones, surgery and most important every trans gender journey of nonsense start from clothing, thanks gender equality people wore in between cloths which is nor for female nor for male and specially females has started wearing male cloths (and trying to do male things) and there is no doubt in that gender dysphoria is more about how one perceive female. And finally, thanks to low testosterone level that transition is partially possible for delusional people's delusion. Generally trans gender take the support of gays and lesbians first let me tell you trans are nonsensical (there is no doubt in that), but same thing we can't say for being gays and lesbian who simply claim to be or are sexually unfit as they are simply sexually unfit either independently or become that by being mentally retard and if unfit on there own- they are at least not driven by blockers, intake of hormones or any kind of surgery or particular clothing and they don't try to become what already exist in a better absolute ways and which can't be relative (or nonsensical in any way), but somebody can be sexually unfit (male or female) because of absolute reasons.

Tough it is hard to say that they (sexually unfit) are real in the sense what they think is driven by just thinking nonsense or something which has is in there base gene (if born fit) because we exactly don't know every cause of being sexually unfit so basically we can't say anything about how and why somebody is or become sexually unfit exactly but homosexuality is ok in the sense of it is not relative bullshit as partial dependency can be formed between any thing but definitely is retarding as it is about sexually unfit people (though the term homo sexual is there to create relative bullshit, just like a person can fuck doll or dildo and call himself or herself doll/dildo sexual, but what I am trying to say is - people indeed become sexually less fit or unfit if born fit without reaching a certain abnormal level like what happens at so-called old age and can have partial dependency with same gender person). But there is no doubt in that the best partial dependency can be formed between male and female only. And there are no doubts gays are just male only and lesbians are female only as they can't be different genders as

1. Partial dependency led to gender formation not gender formation take place first to have partial dependency which is obvious (basically some partial dependency lead to or become dependency and then make sure that certain partial dependency is better to have).

2. Gays and lesbian produce same sperm and oocyte which is there to show who should show partial dependency to whom for reproduction hence gays and lesbians are no other gender and they are just sexually unfit (or may very less fit) because they are not overall for whatsoever reason whether hormones or any thing else not producing kids (if a person doesn't produce sperm or oocyte is not a third gender as it would be direct relative bullshit). One thing to be clear about making yourself sexually or physically unfit because of being mentally unfit (or crazy retard) is just crazy more retardness and that person can't be a thinker, normal or default and is purely worthless. One thing to be clear about less fit is not unfit and unfit is purely absolute which is defined by absolute things for example if you can't move your body or you just can't have kids you purely physically or sexually unfit but if you have little bit less muscle or less flexible let say a deviation of 10% from average fit male or female then you are less fit physically and if you have less or more of a hormone so that you can't have kids on your own directly easily as deviation is up to 50% then you are less fit sexually.

3. When a characteristic is more or less profound it doesn't create a new characteristic or make itself different in any other senses.

4. There is no such thing like 50-50 for considering different combinations of different configuration. Hence every so-called intersex (bullshit term) is either an unfit male or unfit female sexually. There can't be bisexual in human being, if you find a person producing both sperm and oocyte or a third kind of gamete then do let me know.

When it come to hormones I want to be clear about one thing female are submissive (it is not recessive specially for being thinker or normal or default) specially because of there hormones and males are dominant specially because of there hormone but it has nothing to with that female will feel sad or have to feel sad because her hormones are like that, as female feel happy or sad when they think it is necessary to feel so which means if female fulfil her necessity according to hormone as it define brain structure and overall system then she will feel happy and same for male. Retard people Who talk about female anatomy, physiology or what so ever does they have read standard books? Do they even done any studies about anything or have to do something to or with anything? Renovated retard talk about science and philosophy without doing any kind of there own research and without any kind of contribution and without reading standard books and talk just base less without any logic except there bullshit relative logic which is retarding like them but off course for retards it seems like a great deal. And the people who think in old time female use to be just dependent on male or mostly male use to live in way more better condition or happy, for them I want to say one thing if that going to be the case no female would ever love a male nor any male would ever love a female nor we would be here as we already talk that love don't exist it is all about partial dependency which shown by both participant of so called love and yes female output overall have been very less compared to male (and still is the case and there output will always be less overall) but that doesn't mean it was nothing nor it means females were not important though most of the population is worthless for progress and always have been.

So basically there is no such thing like equality, what people do in the name of equality is that they create relative or relative bullshit, every thing has different value so things are not equal nor they can be. The only thing which so-called equality can lead to is survival of unfit. Let me take an example to show how big bullshit equality is and why retards should whipped out fast, the example is the decline in testosterone, sperm count and other male hormone related thing whether any serum related hormone or anything else (we are taking sexually fitness because it is very important but if you sexually fit that no way means you are not retard), now basically if we take same decline rate which will never happen as through natural selection the best will be selected as I told you earlier successful people have high testosterone so you can understand that obvious but for an instance I take that scenario of same decline than let me tell you within next 90 years having a kid will become difficult commodity and after that just in 90-100 years nobody will able to have kid that's it human race will be finished in 180-190 years the race which is running at least of least more than 40000-45000 and even we consider civilisation at least 20000 and again as I told you when people go more retard more nonsense they create and more retardness they show which overall retard the progress. You can check decline of hormones optimization (physical and sexual fitness) is parallel to rise of nonsense which means it has check points of 1950, 1980 and then 2003-2004 (though projection of population is not on the bases of compounding nor most of the population is born unfit on its own), these are the point after which people go crazy more and more retard specially because there is more progress but yet option to live like a retard.

From all this you can understand what should be whipped out was really not got whipped out in terms of people and retardness, that how retarding equality relative or relative bullshit is and let me tell you hormones depends lots on persons direct doings but now today people not to prefer to say people are unfit they just can't say shit to shit (retarding) because most of the population is shit but for sure most of the men and women are really not the fit but instead they just put blame on chemicals, riches, this and that, but let me tell you an example the most male sex hormone depend on (if you are not born unfit) one thing (the most important) in very simple words how much you fuck, how much you interact with beautiful fit female and how risky/adventurous you are, if you do these thing it will give rise to cascade effect more you do them more testosterone will increase to be maintained in optimal range which make you do more of that kind of things and so on. Today retard think people do more sex but let me tell the reality is after marriage sex is declining very fast not only that before marriage is decline very fast too. And again, just to remind you most of the population is not born unfit but becomes unfit and biggest reason for crazy unfit to be born is unfit peoples have kids together but today population is so big that it's number only is crazy retardness. Remember here we have just considered some sex hormone what about other things, how much unfit and retarding most people are?

A example of cascade retardness which is caused by equality relative or relative bullshit is let's say there is polices and subsidies which pushes farmers to produce more food (specially it can be particular food) and directly reducing the cost of food which both in turn reduces the cost of food like crazy for the retard people who also directly get polices and subsidies for the same and also because food was cheaper than standard already they will eat more and more they eat more fat they become and overall unhealthy they become, then they will ask for healthcare and because they will get bit healthcare because of polices and subsidies meanwhile they will get an change to show more retardness like saying I am retard I can't do job or may be because of witch magic I can't get job put me on a payroll then meanwhile then person will have kids, so you know so on it goes. Another example for the same can be taking money from the people which they could have invested to create better infrastructure for there personal security but instead using that to make sure more retard survive, then instead to reducing the retardness directly retards claim that another system on that would be lot more helpful like having more police and policing (and obviously wasting more money in related infrastructure) – which is obviously going to be just more retarding as first being an police officer at best can be about barely coping up with the progress and top of increasing the size of that menial market while it is obvious better defaults would never would like to be a police officer and it is also obvious when there is more retard and menial way of selection what majority of policer officer will be like, so to claim to reduce that retardness then they try to have idiots like politicians to have more rules, laws, regulation and then obviously more judges (and infrastructure related to that to waste more money) who them self are no better (again increasing the size of market which can't do more progress and obviously while having the support of worthless majority) and then these thing just goes on and on (also in many different ways).

At last I just want to say that if scenarios are equal you don't have to make them equal in any way and if two whole scenario are overall equal then overall results would be equal too but if thing are not equal then you can't make them equal, if things which are unequal whether a scenario or a particular thing which can't change as something just can't be equal because they are simply not equal and can't change to become equal for example you or a person himself/herself can't change an old retard (though anybody but other young can have scope of changing) into thinker or normal or default so to become equal to any thinker or normal or default.

Chapter 11

Democracy – Rule of Renovated Retards

The democracy nonsense is favourite of retards because while using that they get lots benefit of the progress and they chose renovated retard to rule who are like them only (which basically doesn't mean anything in terms of progress it is just more retardness), and is favoured by lot of renovated retards as they also get lot of stuff and also an opportunity to rule. The word democracy only popup in the retards mind when they what to create more nonsense and want everything even though they do nothing or simply want to have more which obviously they doesn't deserve and top of all to create laws (all of which I already told you why they make laws) but the most important thing the word democracy don't pop in theses lump and bump heads when they follow one particular religion, renovated retard, and now when they use social media they don't think of democracy, when they post things on internet they don't think of democracy, when they watch bullshit movies and listen bullshit music they don't think of democracy, these worthless peoples don't think about democracy to know how worthless they are, when these retard become retard at that time they don't think of democracy, when they retard the progress they don't think of democracy (as democracy is supposedly to be about freedom but then freedom to do stuff to be better should lead more progress not retard). The one thing to be clear about is freedom means you are free mentally and physical to create particular stuff but it not about not doing any particular stuff or doing nothing (obviously a relative bullshit) which mean if you are a retard, you can't be free whether you under democracy delusion or something else and if you really are a thinker or normal you are free whether you under democracy or something else but obviously you have to tolerate some nonsense and retardness of retards if there is a government.

Now let see from where the democracy starts for retards? It starts right from election from where they chose renovated retard, how bullshit it is calling somebody capable of governing any thing on the basis of whom majority have chosen while knowing most of people are nothing more than retard even if that's not the case still it's idiotic, it's very easy to know how most of people are retard as at the time of election as you on your own can observe most of people talk about parties or renovated retard or some another kind of relative bullshit and you must forget about finding people who talk about new ideas, thoughts, creations etc. (Which doesn't include concept of more), after that these renovated retards who got selected, they decide what to do who don't know anything about anything to do progress, who have created nothing more than bullshit or relative bullshit or relative and there is no doubt in that these renovated retards have nothing to do with progress (which we already talked about) and obviously they want to have more popularity which is obviously about talking more nonsense and showing more retardness for overall progress. So basically, present day so-called democracy or ruling is nothing more than rule of renovated retard and election is nothing more than opt from retards, by the retards and for the retards.

Now one may ask what a better so-called democracy or ruling should be like then here are some points to consider to remove some of the retardness.

1. Every candidate who want to stand in election should have personal success by which I mean that person must have created or modified something, if not then get out (Though right now even very lower end of defaults are better).

2. Every candidate should have knowledge of science and especially biology.

3. Candidate should not be follower of anything particular concept just because that is what his/her convention says as we all know conventional wisdom is not all useful as it is relative bullshit based on past and past is past not present so today's reality is different and real science doesn't change.

4. Even though if you say we can't remove the process of selection through majority we can still remove some nonsense and retardness by doing first 3 things and one more simple thing that every contestant for election should put forward there whatsoever ideas (if have nothing of his/her own should not able to participate) at the same time without knowing what others are putting forward and can't use the relative and more concept and then these should be present to people without people knowing which party and which person has put forward which one and then people should select particular ideas which will reveal which party has

gain majority of votes after that another community should made by the same way not from parties but any person who has personal success can participate to be a person for that community and then that community would analyse the best two ideas which people have selected out that which one is really more useful and progressive in better terms would be selected.

5. Making sure money rolling in name of taxes should be less than 20% of GDP if not immediate action should be taken in a year to make that happen and if country have debut more than 72% then first all the spending should be decreased by at least 20% on yearly bases to pay it off.

6. Reducing money rolling on name of taxes at least by 2% to make sure it become less than 10% of GDP within 3 decades.

7. Politicians should not to be allowed to promise more than 20% of GDP in any polices or subsides at any given moment to be paid in future like pensions whether it will be paid (or not) after 10, 20... or so years and overall, any given period that promise of fund should not be more than 72% of GDP if so, already then, they should be cancelled immediately for most part (like so to make 35%) and then overall it should be reduced slowly to be below 20% within 3 decades.

8. At least for 20% of money from top 20% of tax payers should be volatile by which I mean that they should be given at least 15-20 broad categories to choose from for which they are allowed to chose in to give there money for certain categories. Though that volatile money should be increased from 20% to 80% within 3 decades.

9. Ditching or not letting politician promote the thinking I will make better decisions for you and you will get more as even if a person is not a retard and does indeed make better decision to cause more progress still it is retardness to say or give retards benefit of the progress or anybody who doesn't cope up with that level of progress.

10. Ditching the thinking of they don't know what they need but they need this.

11. Ditching the thinking famous or majority thinking in any way mean more that what it is i.e., thinking which included delusion, ignorance, and overall retardness for most part. And remember when majority is retard and is the problem, it is absurd to say it will become famous and will be in majority thinking that that's the case.

Note – One thing to remember no currency or relative or relative bullshit or bullshit can change what earth is, what carrying capacity is (we are way overpopulated) and that's why majority right not going to get everything or majority of the stuff irrespective of what ever renovated retard says or suggest. One more thing that is very straight forward about governments – they are retarding system, so if any system like that exist it just going to cause retardness (if you are delusional about it's not being retarding or you just directly say so then for sure you are a retard who get's benefit of the progress because of them). One may ask what it is the most retarding thing about governments and how it's very existence or implication is retarding? I think answer is quite obvious, taxes are the most retarding and there very implication is retardness, what government do after that money came in on the name of taxes is just more retardness (they are designed in such to show more retardness) and I can sum that up in one very simple statement i.e., taxes on any particular field or domain or any thing just reduces that thing both quality and quantity wise (and I am well aware that there idiots especially so-called economist who can't understand the difference between lump-sum buying or subscription versus taxes).

Now above things sound like something like progressive to you or anybody but it is not freedom nor progressive but definitely are less retarding which in turn help to maintain progress and which in turn help to do more progress. But still what we talked about will never properly going to happen because even defaults doesn't want to take part in election and one default can't change every thing to very less retarding and remove all nonsense, but obviously better than renovated retard. Thinkers governing are just not an option because the reason is if real thinker would propose any thing that would for sure will contain removal of most of the laws, policies, subsidies etc. which is obviously are very retarding (which obviously are for retards survival) because of which retards never will want a thinker to be elected nor a thinker will ever stand, being elected is just not possible (and obviously that why that never happened otherwise retards would not be here today, especially as majority). Either we can apply the above things or one day (after 2050, especially after 2080) abrupt change would happen causing way more chaos and may bit of retardness at that instance, not only that right now taking those action will definitely reduce the retardness which in turn will help in maintaining progress which in turn will help in doing more progress.

As I said above thing is not real freedom nor an progressive system, if will be there when there would no governing party, no government and people just work together (as 100% population would be thinker, normal and defaults) to led progress and the reality is no progress has ever done in any country because they have better government but progress is always done on the basis of which country has better thinker and normal and how many of them and specially number of defaults which is highly dependent on retard population as they hinder the direct connection of thinker and normal to people to make them defaults or better defaults, more of them more the progress and more of menial pattern following retards (religious shit) in a country less the progress, it is very simple (though government can be more or less retarding which can decide over progress level very prominently). Most important point to understand is corruption happen when competition is low not visa versa first and it is not the biggest problem, obviously biggest problem is most of the population is retard (and we are way over populated) which is obviously the cause of all retardness. But this scenario of no government can only be achieved when there going to be less than 20% retards in the population which will lead to no retards and as there will no retards there will be no renovated retards too. Right now, I think no of millionaire in the world has almost crossed 50 million (more than 56 million as per latest update) so I think there can be a world with population of 2 billion and at least 500 million millionaire and other 1.5 to be rich (according to upper class of so-called rich countries today) too till the early next century (according to today's standards) and off course there will be less than 20% retard population.

One thing to be very clear about democracy never can be freedom or lead to freedom as it is a system of ruling (if freedom is about being progressive). I think one of most famous nonsense is democracy is different from monarchy and specially lot better (or even progressive), answer to that is absolutely no both are simply the same system categorically and overall are the rule of renovated retard (and I know idiots just don't get it, that it doesn't matter how a system is formed, though both are formed in almost the same way indirectly or directly). The only thing about democracy stands out is people have less envy and jealousy and try to have way more things which obviously doesn't change the system (more or less has nothing to do with category) and that is only possible by increasing the system size which is way more retarding. To support the above thing, I will simply make a comparison table which is as follows -

Democracy	Monarchy
In democracy a country is ruled by a president or prime minister that is	In monarchy a country is ruled by kings and queen and they elect people

elected by the people and other people who are elected by elected people like prime minster or president and visa versa through election, which is an government, which is the ruling party, which is supported by majority.	and visa versa who basically rule which is a government only and the right to rule is as king or queen is said to be passed down through a dynasty rather than election (which is at least relative), but Monarch is always supported by majority otherwise it falls just like democracy. So, system wise it is exactly the same.
Ruling party or people are renovated retards not thinker or normal. More number of renovated retards get change to rule but that doesn't change the system as it is about category of people ruling.	Ruling party or people are renovated retards not thinker or normal. Less number of renovated retards get change to rule but that doesn't change the system as it is about category of people ruling.
Majority nonsense prevails.	Majority nonsense prevails.
Most of population is retard but still gets benefits. More or less doesn't matter for category.	Most of population is retard but still gets benefits. More or less doesn't matter for category.
No way promotes science instead of that promote retardness of majority and majority is retard.	No way promotes science instead of that promote retardness of majority and majority is retard.
Claims everybody will be treated equally which is impossible so that doesn't happen.	Doesn't claim everybody will be treated equally which obviously happens.
The very existence of this system is wastage of money.	The very existence of this system is wastage of money.
Laws and polices are made by the people who are supported by majority.	Laws and polices are made by the people who are supported by majority.

Democracy – Rule of Renovated Retards

People give feedback on laws, polices etc. And their feedback can lead to change of laws, polices etc.	People give feedback on laws, polices etc. And their feedback can lead to change of laws, polices etc.
Helps in the survivals of retard which retards the progress and also make sure retards have generations after generations without any direct check.	Helps in the survivals of retard which retards the progress and also make sure retards have generations after generations without any direct check.
The system is not there to create something new or modify something but progress still happens as it has to do with the people who does create something new or modify something and cope up with progress.	The system is not there to create something new or modify something but progress still happens as it has to do with the people who does create something new or modify something and cope up with progress.
At best system just work as a distributor of things (which they didn't created) to retards and renovated retards while destroying the money (which rolled in on the name of taxes or simply the overall wealth) by show crazy retardness.	At best system just work as a distributor of things (which they didn't created) to retards and renovated retards while destroying the money (which rolled in on the name of taxes or simply the overall wealth) by show crazy retardness.
System is not based on progress but overall retard the progress, specially in particular fields.	System is not based on progress but overall retard the progress, specially in particular fields.
The system is the most retarding system as they keep getting at least same amount of money irrespective of how much retardness they show (though generally system gets more and more money while showing more and more retardness at any overall	The system is the most retarding system as they keep getting at least same amount of money irrespective of how much retardness they show (though generally system gets more and more money while showing more and more retardness at any overall

period of decades) and they are the biggest system in any country.	period of decades) and they are the biggest system in any country.
Claims to make investments which one day going to pay off but obviously that doesn't happen because it's a retarding system and that's why ask for more and more money (and get it) mostly by simply taking same percentage out of GDP (which is generally less than 40%). But obviously mostly it is just about Ponzi scheme.	Claims to make investments which one day going to pay off but obviously that doesn't happen because it's a retarding system and that's why ask for more and more money (and get it) mostly by simply taking same percentage out of GDP (which is generally less than 20%). But obviously mostly it is just about Ponzi scheme.
Even though the system is retarding it can be less or more retarding, if less retarding than it helps in maintaining certain progress which in turn helps in doing more progress. But obviously system doesn't lead progress. Generally, this is more retarding simply because it's a reference to bigger system.	Even though the system is retarding it can be less or more retarding, if less retarding than it helps in maintaining certain progress which in turn helps in doing more progress. But obviously system doesn't lead progress. Generally, this is less retarding simply because it is a reference to smaller system.

Chapter 12

What Now?

This is the most important question i.e., what now? First enjoy the doom of retards and retardness, second transformation will happen we are going to go through it but we still are not at transitional state it will take at least 25-30 years to perfectly on transitional state and just like every transitional state it will of short period of time and it will be the peak of all nonsense but after that the best will be there for humans (obviously for the progressive ones) in terms of progress and happiness as progress leads to happiness or we can say it is happiness in it self too.

Thing we have discussed in here in this book and what gone crazy retarding and what can be done will more applicable to make new laws, system, better world and creating absolute, not only that we also understood what is nonsense and how retarding it is. For progress one must not ignore and one should not ignore his or her necessities which is the ultimate most important reality and one must remember while doing anything that it will shape his/her necessities so one must ask himself/herself how at the moment before start doing that thing - going affect me mentally and physically, small change in necessities continuously create a significant change in necessity (comparative to whole necessity in particular and as whole). One must focus on knowledge not just information and one should be an absolutist, and again you feel happy or sad when you think it is necessary to feel so (everything is about stuff).

There is nothing like procrastination or priorities, a person do what he/she think is necessary to do at the moment that's why your are doing what you are doing at the moment because nobody can do unnecessary things and there is nothing like lateral thinking or critical thinking or thinking out of the box because you just can't think of something unnecessary or non connected to what you think is necessary and there is nothing like serendipity. At last if you think every thing happen to you because some bullshit or relative bullshit higher being (or any other hollow term) is watching you, then let me tell you every thing happen to you because you are not the only living being in this world nor you are living in a void. Remember you can't think unnecessary nor you can do unnecessary nor you can do unnecessary to anybody else nor anybody can think unnecessary nor anybody can do unnecessary nor they can do unnecessary to you so unnecessary never happens (again everything is about stuff).

But before we end this book, I want you to understand a very simple pyramidal graph (Maslow's hierarchy of needs, given on this page) which I think is quite famous, to understand why it is retardness, worthless for any kind of progress and why it makes necessities and overall categorization a relative bullshit.

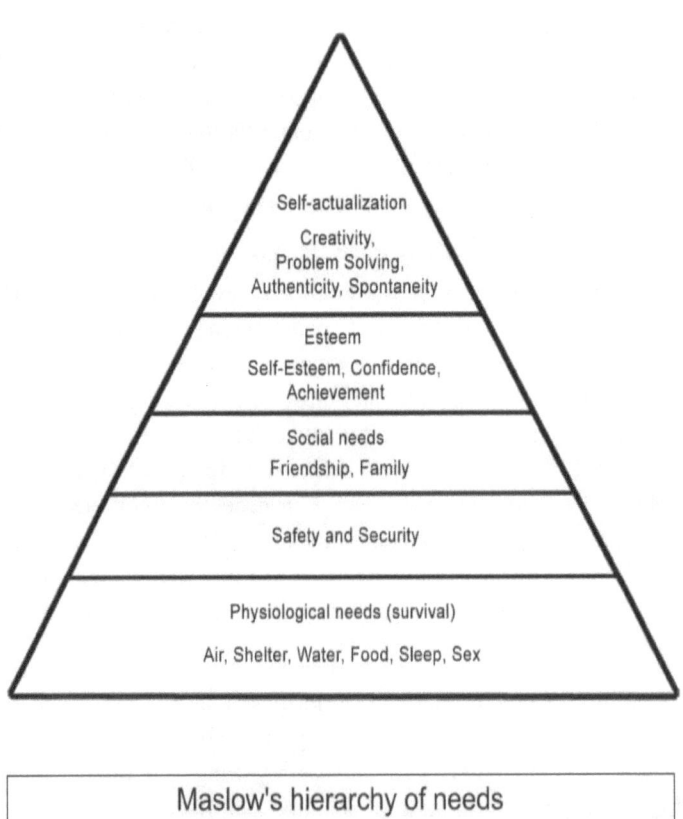

Maslow's hierarchy of needs

What Now?

Though it is obvious Maslow's is a pyramidal graph and there is no such thing like a necessity coming first and coming last for overall survival, this graph should be at least a set graph something like given on this page, so that it can be absolute not relative. But then also it is very important to understand that it is nonsense to say survival without getting benefits of the progress (and in ideal world where there is no retardness retards would not exist because of that very fact).

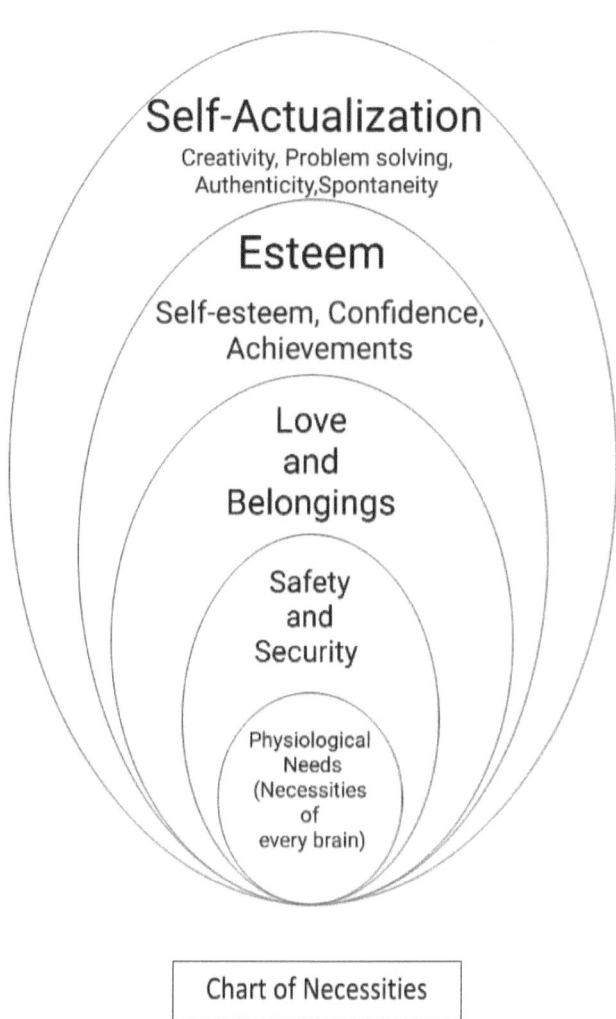

Chart of Necessities

Now let's understand the chart of necessity and problem with Maslow's hierarchy of needs. First thing first if you are thinker or normal or default you are on the self-actualization (by your own i.e. you get benefit of progress because you are overall progressive), if you are renovated retard you are on esteem column (not own your own) , if are a retard you can be at any of other three columns(not own your own), so overall basically person who survive should survive and would survive only because that person is getting benefits of the progress (progress which is result of self actualization) but definitely retards exist otherwise basically everything is one and same but just different configuration but not an different category hence we will vanish the line in between for people (hence also be busting hierarchy of needs).

The column of self-actualization and esteem can be one and only as whether confidence, achievements or self esteem all depends on self-actualization only (as name suggest too) without that there can't be esteem but renovated retards have all of the esteem (delusion) on the bases of followers which is indeed is about the following not about a particular thing because they didn't created any progressive thing at the first place (and also there achievements of increasing following doesn't lead to progress but just more retardness) and because of that they get's the benefits of the progress, all which is not from self actualization so basically there esteem is based on an delusion (relative bullshit) so basically you can break there esteem (delusion) just by take there followers down. Therefore person can't have esteem without having self actualization for himself/herself and for his/her creation (not necessarily being an thinker is necessary).

Till now you may have understood why most of the population brag about love and belongings because they are retards. Thinker, normal and defaults doesn't brag about love and belonging as they are have that being progressive from which I mean - for example, this book is written by me for sure it is my belonging but right now also I am not afraid of loosing it nor I would brag about it as after all this book is written by me I am creator I can create again what I have created once and of course thinkers and normal can create new and new things again and again but also the people get the knowledge of certain stuff. Now if it is the question about love I already told you it can't be more than partial dependency but of course the people who brag about it is simply the people who again are not the creator but just got into partial dependency once (because of very few reason specially for retards it s just that little bit new generally another retard person but obviously retards just go more retard not better nor newer version of them self) but again can't get into that again and again or just can't maintain it as I told you it has to be continuous which in itself means progressive not stuck about one thing which simply just bragging about particular belonging which only progressive people can do (remember mostly retard people lie about more love or belonging or basically create an relative bullshit on the name of them and whatever bit they get they got it from benefits of progress), hence love and belonging is also about self actualization.

Now you may ask why graph like that? though this graph is accurate except people would be claiming to be at any column other than self actualization would be not be having that column things instead would be bragging about that to have as without self- actualization people can't have anything properly and specially not more than sort period of time specially as species without it (i.e. getting benefit of the progress) and thus renovated retards and retards are always miserable. You can understand that without self-actualization you can't have real esteem and without self-actualization you can't maintain and have partial dependency and really you can't have belonging until and unless you are a progressive person. And you can't have safety and security without problem solving, creativity and spontaneity. At last, you can't have fulfilment of all common necessities of every brain until and unless you are (more) creative as specially because of the importance of new and cope up with the progress (authenticity has nothing to do with anything while fulfilling necessity as it is just a result of comparison and obviously its take lot more to create something new but way less to learn that new thing because it is what it is which can be used wherever it can be used by anybody). So overall to maintain all of necessities fulfilment and one have to have self- actualization, hence indeed being retard you can't live (survive) but then retards survive even there are highly miserable and exist today because thinker, normal and defaults existed and exist and they (retards) get their progress benefits for so-called free. The biggest delusion of retards which make them more retard and retard the progress the most is there can be survival (and continuation of things) without progress whether it is in the form of they think they can survive without it or they don't get it at the first place or they should be getting it because of some nonsense or anything else.

"Whether you work for fulfilling all of your necessities or not still it will not change the fact you have necessities, if you fulfil your necessities then it is a necessity in itself and even you don't work to fulfil all of your necessities that also going to be part of your necessity only, which you have created yourself for suffering"

www.ingramcontent.com/pod-product-compliance
Lightning Source LLC
LaVergne TN
LVHW041610070526
838199LV00052B/3079